Tan Rai

"Diary of a Special Forces A-Team Commander in Vietnam"

June 1966 to March 1967

Raymond JStriler

Written by:
Ray J. Striler, Ed. D.

CONTENTS

AUTHORS NOTE

These daily entries are left as they were written in 1966-67 except for clarification. The theme reflects my search for meaning. I judiciously left out classified materials, emotive situations, the gory and grotesque. Mainly because most Survival Assistance Officers upon death will hide such pictures and writings from loved ones. It was the macho thing to do, just as it was 'macho' to be overly zealous with firepower. Substantiating and supporting material has been added that I gathered from conversations with those in the book and classified materials that have since been declassified. I am proud of my service with Special Forces. It was a powerful experience. One of exhilaration, frustration, sorrow, self-discovery, sagacity, survival, growth, education, love, and respect of people. A war zone is a collage of planned and unplanned activity that taxes emotion, survival, intellect, the sixth sense, values, and growth. I have not since had experiences whereby my endorphin and adrenaline levels have fluctuated up and down my spine so precipitously. I was 27 years old during that tour, astonishingly, older than most. This diary is laid out much like a Special Forces operation. Since we built our camp from scratch the sequence parallels Special Forces classical doctrine. First we find the indigenous natives, in this case, the Montagnards. We recruit, organize, equip, train, fight, and retain the force. During this specific time we built a Special Forces A-Team Camp, we conducted squad, platoon, company and battalion-sized operations against the Vietcong and North Vietnamese Army (NVA); we incorporated lessons learned, and became culturists. This is about leadership of a small elite American unit advising an elite Vietnamese unit and leading a large and wonderful tribe of Nomadic Montagnard spiritual tribesmen, the K'ho.

Our story is that of a handful of dedicated professionals fighting to prevent communism in a strange and distant land. It is a story of military missionaries (not mercenaries) willing to give our lives in order to help an oppressed people. Later in life I met Father Norman Muckerman who had a similar mission during the exact same time however, he was in the Amazon. He was a Catholic Redemptorist priest on a mission from God. The similarities in task however are striking. We were idealists. We were similar to the Peace Corps carrying an M16. Father Muckerman carried the cross. Our leader, President Kennedy gave the impetus to the Peace Corps appointing his own brother in law, Sergeant Schriver, as director just as he gave the impetus to the Green Berets when he told General Yarborough, at Fort Bragg, NC, to wear the green beret and be proud. We loved and respected the people, the land and the culture of the Vietnamese and Montagnards. Ours was not a world of Saigon corruption or Washington DC politics; ours was a world of pioneers willing to live and eat and fight with local indigenous people in hopes of a better way of life for the children. I was more of a Redemptorist Priest than a steely-eyed trained killer yet, I had been trained for six years how to kill and manage violence and chaos. This small voice will tell how we went to Vietnam not to destroy, but to build a nation based on truth, justice and democracy. Ours was a mission of peace like our founder, Colonel Aaron Bank, repeated on many occasion. It was our duty, our honor our country and our brothers for whom we fought. The Special Forces motto is "de oppresso liber" meaning "freedom for the oppressed." That was the American Way; the right thing to do in view of the times and belief that communism was spreading throughout South East Asia.

This is just my perspective. There were 12 wonderful A team members assigned to Tan Rai who did far more than I could ever have done. It would take volumes to describe the good they did. They accomplished so much for the beloved Montagnards that went unseen and unnoticed. Believe me the people of the land appreciated it, I appreciated it. I was honored to be in the company of such noble warriors.

I commanded a Special Forces A-Team for over eight months. The A-Team commander was a high risk and low paying occupation. So why did I do it? I seem to recall it was the most exciting and most patriotic thing to do at the time.

Carlsbad, California
Ray Striler Ed. D.

AKNOWLEDGEMENT

Special Dedication to Charles "Chuck" Orona, our team medic. Fortunately we were able to get together in the years after this diary was written. He passed away in 1998 after a bout with Cancer, which happened to be the same year I returned to Vietnam after 32 years. It is in his memory that this book is written and dedicated. He wrote a paragraph after reading my draft. It was much more articulate and picturesque than mine. It can be read at Appendix 2.

Tan Rai is also dedicated to Wells E. Cunningham, Commander at Duc Co A-253 best friend Appendix 3, Jimmy Coleman, my first cousin, Captain Wilbanks (USAF), FAC pilot and friend (Medal of Honor recipient posthumously, See Appendix 4) plus other fallen comrades who ultimately sacrificed their lives for our freedom.

Thanks to, Edward "Ned" McGonagle, Sam Lien Le, Clyde Sincere, Carl Schneider, Steve Sherman, Jim Humphries, Mary Lou Darnell, Rob Harder, Jim Nabors, Chet Jones, Bobby Clark, Hans Gross, Bo Baker, Roger Donlon, Bob Williams, Howard Louderbach, Mary Roebling, Eric Eskam, Ann & Bill Lacy, Bobby & Brent Darnell, Jimmie, Debi, Tammy and Adam Striler, John and Mendy Lewis and Bud Gillette, for encouraging me to publish this diary.

Not to forget, Khiet Truong, Son Nguyen, Matt Dansbury, Roland Miraco, Dick Bouchard, Dane Tkacs, Bob Karmazin, Bob Kvederas, Bill Hampton, Aaron Bank, Bob Charest, Terry Klinger, Les Crow, Jeff Gibson, Jim Richie, Bob Greene, Lee Wilson, Paul Hoffner, Jim Lennox, Bruce McMillan, Marvin Ozley, Jeffrey Roberts, Pat Baker, Robert Tink and Ken Zike.

A very heartwarming thanks to my mom for bringing awareness to the imprint I make upon people. Thanks to my brothers Bill and Curly and my little sister Mary Lou for their special encouragement, love and support.
A special thanks to my wonderful family, Heidi, Alex, Mike and Rob and their families for their continuous encouragement and support. May the little ones, Summer, Karina, Lexi, Cole, Zach and Will read this with pride.
A special thanks to Alex for his meticulous editing.

SECTION ONE: TAN RAI SPECIAL FORCES A-TEAM

CHAPTER 1 INDIGENOUS NATIVES

June 27, 1966 Tan Rai A-Team My first day on the job as an A-Team Commander. What a glorious and proud day. I still can't believe it. All my dreams have come true. All the preparation, work, sweat, and tears have led me to this moment of challenge. As I walked the Tan Rai Special Forces A-Team camp perimeter earlier this morning to inspect the mines, the claymores, booby-traps, wire and weapons, the rain came down profusely blurring my vision making me more acutely aware of my inner desire to be conscious of all excruciating details. The animal instinct in me is becoming more acute and dominant after four months in country. I feel the closeness to nature as if I am an integral part of it. The temperature is cold and the rain pushes the chill to the bone. I am in command. I feel the authority and awesome burden of responsibility placed upon my shoulders for all the people in my Area of Operations (AO). In observing the English language classes for the Montagnard children this evening, I saw the eagerness on their happy little faces. One would not guess we are in a War Zone and smack in the middle of the Ho Chi Minh Trail extension. The volunteer participation was tremendous. I believe these people have more of an aptitude for English than we have for their language, or is it that they are more motivated? Their total vocabulary probably consists of 500 words.

The 'Yards' willingness to learn was evident. Sergeant First Class Barnes, a strong gentle instructor, would call someone to the blackboard and recite the numbers in English or say a few phrases. To my amazement they were surprisingly accurate and quick to catch on. They want to learn, English. They love the Americans. We are compared to the French whom they also admired. It is mutual admiration. Barnes is a big strapping strong good-natured Heavy Weapons Sergeant, who generally keeps to himself. Very confident yet to avoid tension he would likely turn away from an argument and go off by himself to meditate. He comes alive teaching the Yards. Being the commander of a Special Forces A Detachment is gratifying and humbling at the same time. This is the job I was trained for. It seems a camp is as good as the imagination of the people running it. I had to give one of my NCO's a direct order this morning to go to Nha Trang to the hospital for an X-ray. He still has shrapnel close to his kidney. He would not have gone on his own. He was worried if he left camp that the workload would build up on the rest of us. That's dedication.

June 28, 1966 **Mission** Our mission is to advise and assist the Vietnamese Special Forces LLDB (VNSF) in the conduct of the Civilian Irregular Defense Group (CIDG) Program. Our CIDG program establishes an Economy-Of-Force mission of local security at the Tan Rai village and hamlet level. We are manned with paramilitary indigenous Montagnard forces, the K'ho tribesmen. We provide early warning of enemy units coming across the Cambodian border into Vietnam. There are 88 CIDG/SF/LLDB camps located throughout the four Corps of Vietnam.

Tan Rai is a typical camp consisting of a 12 man United States Special Forces (USSF) A-Team of two officers and 10 enlisted men augmented by a Psychological Operations and Civil Affairs officer, our VNSF counter parts, approximately five CIDG 90 man CIDG light infantry companies, and several 40 man reconnaissance platoons for a total of approximately 580 soldiers.

CIDG personnel, my Montagnard troops, are recruited from local ethnic populations; in our case the K'ho tribe is in the environs around Tan Rai. We allow them to stay close to their families and homes. A five-year enlistment is equivalent to equal service in the regular VN Army (ARVN), thereby avoiding the "draft". We issue the latest U.S. weapons available, Carbines. We pay a salary plus bonus for combat, capture of weapons and we offer medical treatment, housing and food.
The K'hos are interested in serving in the CIDG because of the American SF involvement. After centuries of abuse and neglect by outsiders and the low-landers, the Vietnamese, the CIDG Program offers recognition and citizenship status. Just as Native American tribes suffered by overwhelming outside changes, so too do the Montagnards have to adapt or perish. Fighting in the CIDG is a matter of survival. Somewhat primitive in their habits, their knowledge of the jungle and mountain terrain makes them prime candidates for an Economy-Of-Force Mission to detect and intercede movement along the Ho Chi Minh trails. In the remote areas, trained Montagnards serve as a trip flag, and thereby allow reaction forces to sweep in and destroy the enemy using tactical maneuvers.

Although there are virtually no American Units in my area of operations (AO) occasionally an ARVN Unit will operate nearby. Accordingly, we send out self-protecting patrols and multi-company sized operations to seek out infiltrators and control the areas around the camp. As these operations become more and more effective, the North Vietnamese are forced to direct their forces to eliminate CIDG (Civilian Irregular Defense Group) Camps.

Tan Rai, in Lam Dong Province at the terminus of II Tactical Corps is about 100 miles from Saigon and 40 miles from Cambodia. Our camp is located astride a major Viet-Cong supply and infiltration route forking off the infamous Ho Chi Minh Trail, which funnels men and materials south into Saigon. We conduct counter-guerrilla operations against local Viet-Cong units and interdict the movement of enemy personnel and equipment throughout our Area of Operations. My Area of Operations (AO) is 7 by 10 miles of canopied jungle and highland rolling hills and waterfalls. It is an older forest and has lots of wildlife such as Tigers and Elephants. Without the war it would be paradise. The terrain has many features that make it ideal for our small agile units. We travel cross-country much quicker than larger, more heavily armed units. In the low area we navigate around the swamps and mangroves and move speedily through higher elevations. If we have to move over high ground and can't travel the ridgelines, our movement is slowed to two hundred to three hundred meters per hour. If there are elephants in the area we use their zigzag trails if they coincided with our route of march. We have a mixture of flora and fauna and terrain in our AO; tea, coffee and rubber plantations, mangrove, nipa, swamp, waterfalls, rivers, streams, palm, pine, bamboo and brushwood but very little clear forest.

Our task is difficult because there is no love lost between the Yards and the Vietnamese lowlanders. The Vietnamese from both sides have victimized Yards, so they mistrust the South as well as the North. However they reserve a special hatred for the North. Because their remote mountain villages often straddled North Vietnamese infiltration routes, they are repeatedly subjected to communist atrocities. Their women are raped, village chiefs beheaded, rice confiscated and their young men forcibly conscripted. Many villages pack up and flee. The K'hos refuse to leave their ancestral homelands and embrace the help we offer. This is the case at Tan Rai.

The sound of their language differs. K'ho language is a mixture of singsong and guttural tones which have a "clippity-clop" quality when they speak.

While making my first visit to the dispensary, I noticed a boy who had a bullet in his head. He was still alive. I held a little Montagnard girl while she had a tooth extracted. Her threshold for pain was higher than mine, as she did not whimper.

I flew around the area of operations today in a small observation airplane piloted by Captain Wilbanks and dropped leaflets in Viet Cong (VC) territory. We were looking for VC activity. The leaflets were of a personal nature. We take pictures of captured Viet Cong and put their picture along with words of encouragement in their own language. We ask them to give up life in the jungle and come to the Chieu Hoi centers for rehabilitation and comfort. This theme should be especially enticing during Monsoon season. I have to keep in mind however, that most are illiterate. I hope the pictures on the leaflets will explain our plea. The Special Forces team arrived at this camp in January 1966, just five short months ago at Special Forces Camp Tan Rai Coordinates: ZT09958765.

They cleared the top of the hill with axes and bulldozers and started building the camp. They recruited, equipped and trained the K'ho Montagnards. Now it is my task to finish building the camp, continue recruiting and to train the fighting force to conduct company-sized operations. My mission is, war by attrition, according to General Westmoreland. My intuition tells me there is more to it than that. I not only have to wage war against the VC but I have to shore up the local economy and make it more credible to join the South Vietnamese cause plus keep it safe for the indigenous.

In addition to command responsibilities, each American is also assigned duties as specialists in one or more areas: operations and intelligence, communications, medical, light weapons, heavy weapons, or demolitions for me its area study, intelligence, leadership and command.

June 29,1966 I flew to Bao Loc, the closest city to my A Detachment of Tan Rai, to confer with the Province Chief and a priest at the Catholic Church. Bao Loc is a wonderful mid-sized town 10 Miles to our south. We drove along the dirt streets, the open-air restaurants, colorful storefronts, and white-plastered villas. We occasionally saw a Catholic Church, reminding us of the French influence. Smells of bougainvillea flowers, spicy Oriental cooking, fish sauce and the noxious belches of diesel fumes announced the center of town. The narrow streets were congested with Cyclos, Bicycles, Vespas, Lambrettas, and Military Vehicles. The streets were surfaced with packed red clay and laterite.

CHAPTER 2 COUNTERPARTS; LLDB

June 30,1966 LLDB is the acronym for Luc Luong Dac Biet. The Vietnamese Special Forces.

I met my Vietnamese counterpart. He looks like a professional who just graduated from the West Point of the Orient, the Vietnamese military academy in Dalat. It was good to get back to the team. They are a great bunch, one of the hardest working, best suited and professional groups with whom I have ever been associated. They remind me of the team I commanded in Germany, A-20, just a few short months ago and the Underwater Recovery Team of Europe.

The Montagnard Striker payday formation is something to behold. Company by company, Montagnard by Montagnard they reported to receive pay, ranging from $18 to $60 a month per family. Their signature is a fingerprint. Some of the women tried to claim more children than they really had. I quickly devised a method to identify the family true headcount. I lined the Strikers, their wives and children up on the airstrip in formation. Then I would go down the line and pay family by family according to how many dependents they had. The children cannot be counted twice this way. Team Sergeant (MSG) Carl Samuleson was juggling three grenades; a white phosphorus "willie -peter", a smoke and a frag, while telling me how much tougher the Korean War was.   Then he reminded me how old he was by saying:

"As soon as I DEROS (Date of Estimated Return from Overseas) to Fort Bragg, I will retire and honcho the bag boy detail at the commissary."

He burst out laughing with a huge infectious belly laugh, which befits his huge stature. I knew he was dead serious. Samualson's job is to lead the enlisted men and provide me guidance. He is like the old man with many years of experience and he coddles his Sergeants like a grandmother.

July 1, 1966 I had another conference with the Catholic priest from Bao Loc. He has agreed to lend me schoolteachers for my Striker village's children. The village, half way down the runway, is where the Strikers and their dependents live. He offered two Catholic Nuns from Bao Loc. I showed him the schoolhouse and equipment. The schoolhouse adjoins my CIDG store and is simply a roof, concrete floor, and walls with no windows. The tables and benches are made of ammo crates. The priest consented to allow the nuns to teach until we refurbish the schoolhouse at Tan Rai at which time they will move into the refurbished one.

July 2, 1966 After having inspected the perimeter with my counterpart, I feel better about this system of advising. We are able to speak openly to each other. He is an impressive, intelligent, proud Vietnamese Officer. He and I are beginning to agree on important issues, especially operations.

July 3, 1966 Later I coordinated operations with the District advisor, Colonel Corcoran from Bao Loc. The pilot, Captain Wesby, drank one cup of Rice Wine and as the lightening liquid burned his throat, he said with a forced smile

"That's *shore* good stuff."

July 4, 1966 I gave the Americans a half-day off. Sergeant Michael G. Krapfl, our medic, made a rocket to commemorate the 4th of July. It just fizzled and flopped. The "Yards" had a good laugh at that!

July 5, 1966 Combat Patrol: I left at 0700 hours this morning on a company-sized combat patrol. I've been under fire before at Duc Co but this was a day of close calls. The "Old Captain, (Dai Uy)", that's me, almost got zapped! I was really lucky because a few rounds were intended for me personally. They were fired from about ten feet and landed zinging just a half-inch over my head, putting a hole in my bush hat. Luckily, Charley got nervous and was a poor shot or I wouldn't be here writing now. Our first contact was at 1120 hours. We were walking on a dirt path with security on both flanks. The left flank security overlooked five Viet Cong laying in hiding where they were in ambush positions along the trail between the security element and me. They had a Chi-com RPD, automatic machine gun, and two carbines. They let thirty men go by them and then opened up on the 31st man, the tall one, me! They were using Guerrilla tactics; Kill the Americans. They waited until they saw a tall one with the "black gun", as they called it. I'm 6' 2" and the Yards are about 5 feet. I stick out like an Elephant in tall grass. I hit the dirt by a banana bush. My M-79 Rocket Launcher man said he saw five VC. I only saw two from my vantage point. They withdrew immediately, which, I think, is partly why they missed me. They were in such a hurry; they probably fired on the run as they withdrew, thereby raising the barrel and, consequently, the trajectory of the bullet. We threw grenades, then pursued them, in vain. We found their camp and location from where they fired, which was just a few meters from me. I still have one of their empty cartridges. It was about ten feet from me. God was protecting me. Thank you, God. My animal instinct caused me to duck just as they fired. My body and mind did it instinctively. A pilot was killed at Tan Rai by lifting his head when the explosion took place.

The next episode happened at 1515 hours. We were waiting for the point squad to complete a reconnaissance of the area that we were to move into. Suddenly our rear squad opened fire. I dashed back to where the firefight was. The company commander ran up to me and handed me a Viet Cong weapon, a PPSH 41 machine gun, and four rucksacks full of medicine. He kept shouting, "beaucoup VC, beaucoup VC!" I motioned for him to go get them and then we all ran at a dead heat after the Cong. It wasn't that easy, there was a pretty good firefight going on at the time. A VC squad cut down on us. I thought at the time it was a platoon because of the heavy volume of fire and the zinging overhead. I hate it when the zinging starts but I am acutely aware of every surrounding twig, branch, log, tree and smell of the battlefield. Everything slows down in your mind.   We fired back on them using, M-79's, grenade launchers, carbines, and M-16s at close range. We killed one VC and wounded others. The Forward Air Controller (FAC) in an Air Force spotter plane was overhead immediately. The pilot was our friend Wesby. I could always count on him. Sure enough his familiar voice gave us the assurance we needed. I called camp to get a platoon out to pick up the captured items so we would not have to return to camp so soon. I knew the VC would try to recapture them. The value amounted to 300,000 piasters ($290) plus several important documents. In other words it was an expensive loss for Charley. That was the first successful operation for this camp since it's beginning. It was the first time to capture a weapon. Everyone was very excited about it, but not as excited as me. It was also the first time to capture medicine. Unfortunately we took one friendly casualty. He received shrapnel in the chest but lived. I sure slept well that night, even though I had guard duty for two shifts of two hours each. There were three Americans on the patrol along with the company of Yards. It's my policy that one American stays awake by the radio at all times. We deserved our sleep. As we chased the VC today it occurred to me later how vulnerable we were running down a trail with no flank security. July 6, 1966 The strangest thing happened today. It highlights the fact that I think I am in touch with my sixth sense at times. We were all perfectly still on the trail thinking the VC where near. I could feel the presence of danger. I looked around and did not see or hear anything, but I knew danger was lurking. Something intuitively told me. Then I raised myself higher and looked down the trail. At the same time a cobra raised its head to look at me. For that moment the cobra and I must have had the same fear of danger near us. Neither could see nor hear but we both sensed each other. It was an incredible and eerie experience. I was in touch with my sixth sense. My survival intuitions were kicking in. Where does my sixth sense come from? Take a journey back with me to get to know my background; I have a heavy Christian influence from my parochial school days. That school emphasized values of truth and hard work. Unconditional positive regard and respect for people came from my family, my mom and dad, brothers and sister and wonderful teachers in elementary and high school. My father died when I was eleven years old so my mother was a great influence during my formative years. I did not become "Self" with a capital "S" until I was about seventeen. I graduated from high school and I hitch hiked with a total of $20 from Missouri to Montana where I worked in the Forest Service. I was on my own. I was making the decisions. I thought it would be hard on my mother at the time, but the greatest adventure was to leave Crystal City Missouri and go to the great adventures beyond. My mother in a loving manner allowed me the freedom to explore life on schedule, a little at a time. She provided the support, which enabled me to handle hurt and failure without losing self-esteem.

We prayed often on our knees as a family and were allowed to express our feelings honestly, without fear of punishment for having feelings. I tested boundaries. I pushed and stretched until I knew my limit and beyond that was God and the unknown.

As a soldier I am constantly asking myself about the right to defend. In Plato's Apology, Socrates reminds us,

"The just man concerns himself far more with whether he does right or wrong than with whether he lives or dies."

I know it was hard on my family to see me go off to Vietnam but my mother, two brothers and sister love and support me in my decision. I feel the same about my new family, Heidi and Alex. They too support my decision.

I told Sam Lien Le, the best translator/interpreter I ever had to go to higher headquarters where it is safer. I heard it through my intelligence network that someone was out to get him besides he is so young and so talented. The B-Team asked for him and I decided to let him go at our expense for the higher purpose. I'm sure Major Gillette will use him wisely on Civil Affairs and Psychological Operations. After all we have to win their hearts and minds as well.

SECTION TWO: BUILDING A CAMP

CHAPTER 3 BUILDING A DEFENSIBLE CAMP

I scooped a small hole in the jungle floor with my Randall knife and buried my plastic rice bag.
"Hand me your chamber brush Larry."
I wanted to impress my Medic that I knew to keep my weapon clean.
Today we only saw two VC. They were out of small arms range. We were adjusting mortar rounds on the VC and a shell came in on our position. Fortunately everyone heard it whistle and all hit the ground. No one was injured. We set up ambushes and waited for Charley. No luck! Griff was showing me the capability of the 4.2 mortar today. He demonstrated mortar-bracketing methods. The first round was long, over the VC. The second was short, between camp and us. Therefore he had the VC bracketed, right? He called the mortar crew and requested them to split the bracket and fire for effect. Just after he called the command in I thought for a minute and looked at him. We both realized simultaneously that he had not only bracketed the VC, but our own position as well. That's why the mortar came in on us. It had our name on it! No one was injured fortunately; don't know about the VC, so we let the VC go for another day. I could almost see them laughing through my binoculars as they ran away confused.

The Montagnards are extremely loyal. When it came time to sleep, they made my bed by stringing my poncho as a hammock without me knowing and positioned themselves on all sides of me for protection. If Charley came after me he would have to kill my bodyguards; four in all. I am developing a genuine love and respect for these Yards. Paradoxically, they are likable, fun loving and at the same time ferocious warriors. They had my coffee ready when I awoke. It surprised me so I drank it even though I normally don't drink much. I don't want anyone waiting on me. They think it's great when I go on operations with them, especially since I carry my own rucksack. K'Gee, the Battalion Commander, said, "Dai Uy, you number one." They are not accustomed to seeing officers go on patrol and rarely see them carrying their own equipment.

I saw a man having an epileptic fit today. My interpreter initially said a snake bit him, so I cut his pants off looking for the bite while the "Bac Xi" (doctor) got his instruments ready for treatment. I was almost sure a poisonous snake had bitten him. We finally figured out that it was an epileptic seizure. He went through some funny contortions and twitching. I then saw another K'ho pinch his forehead and neck, until the blood flowed, to let the evil spirits out. My "Bac Xi" put a halt to that. The Yards believe in that type medicine as much as we believe in penicillin.

July 7, 1966 We looked around at daybreak and saw nothing, so we came back to camp after an exhausting operation. We stopped off at the river and grenaded the fish so we would have fresh fish for dinner. The reception by the Montagnards was like a presidential reception. All the villagers lined up on the fence. All the Strikers cheering and finally the Americans to greet us.

The team members called a formation, took pictures and presented Sergeant Larry with a phony "purple heart" because a piece of shrapnel from the M-79 hit him on the cheek and ripped part of his cheek off. It was sure good to get back to camp.

Vanhorne is smart, witty, strong and very competent in medicine and always has a story to tell based on "experience". Each time the story gets better with embellishment. He plays tricks on his fellow soldiers. Like calling them into the mortar pit and dropping a round in the chamber when they are not looking. The blast incessantly rings their ears and enrages them (us). He is overly concerned about his receding hairline. He rubs his head as if to hide it while preparing you for a quip or a story or a gag of his experiences. People enjoy him and want to befriend him as soon as they meet him. Over the course of the next few weeks I expect to talk to each member of the team and get individual views on how to fight this war. SP4 (Specialist 4th Class) Eugene A. Tafoya had an interesting perspective on how Recondo should operate. He suggested that we dress up in VC uniforms, walk down the trail and when close enough grenade them. His blue eyes got larger and larger as his white receding forehead reddened along with his ears as he got to the punch line.

"Then you blow the little bastards to smithereens."

July 8, 1966

I flew to Buon Ma Thuot with my team sergeant, Master Sergeant Samualson, for an A-Team commander's conference. On the way we talked about leadership. He asked me what my leadership philosophy was.

I told him it depended on the situation but as the chopper blades wopped on and drowned out any conversation, I thought to myself;

'I look for harmony, unity, and above all progress. I have transcended selfishness and Narcissism on the path toward amour-propre or self-confidence. I understand paradoxically that I get most by giving. I have found this in teachings of the Upanishads, the Gospels, the Vedas, Socrates, Bhagavad Gita, Goethe, Feuerbach, Rogers and all my mentors. I am not autocratic or directive. For example, I tell the cook what to do and when to do it and give him the tools. I suggest to my colleagues what my philosophy is on a matter and how we can work toward the realization of that concept. Mine is, "Embrace the moment and trust my instincts."

As I finished my thought process, we were landing in Buon Ma Thuot. Top nodded and said,

"Let's go to the meeting" as if he was bored stiff.

The B team conference is for all six A-Team commanders in the Buon Ma Thuot AO (B-23) to get together and get guidance from the boss, Major Edward "Bud" C. Gillette III. It is exciting for me as it is my first meeting here as a commander rather than a staff officer. I had spent a few months here as the Intelligence Officer where I read extensively about FULRO (Unified Front for the Liberation of Oppressed Peoples). I interviewed FULRO officers.

After the conference, Dave Johnson, my food contractor, invited Captain John H. Jackson (A-234 Lac Thien), Captain William D. Daniels Jr. (A-233 Bu Prang) Trang Phuc or as we called it Buon Ea Yong), and me over for Chinese food. The six-course dinner was delicious. I still don't know what all I ate. I recall a few small eyeballs but they were hot and spicy, delicious and deep-fried. I'm sure the third course was dog. I'm getting pretty good with chopsticks.

There was a report in mid June that two fresh NVA regiments moved into the Central Highlands from Laos to serve as the Vanguard for an upcoming enemy offensive. I have no direct indication that they are in our area yet. Maybe out West or North West? It does seem like there is more activity but I can't prove it.

According to the paper, Premier Ky and Chief of Staff Thieu are calling for sterner military measures, including a land invasion of North Vietnam. Now that's the right idea. Ky is urging an allied invasion of North Vietnam even at the risk of a military confrontation with Communist China. I like this idea for a change. It's a statement of resolve. He is, however a paper tiger, in my opinion, the master of rhetoric. The problem is that his rhetoric is not congruent with his actions. I remember last week he was verbally accosting the Buddhist who had allegedly risen up against him. His actions show his insecurity.

July 9, 1966 We cover a lot of information at these B-23 meetings; friendly and enemy situation, logistics, communications, awards and tactical and strategic operations. During the breaks I get to talk to my fellow A-Team Commanders. Compared to them, I have few problems.

Captain Donald H. Sweigart and I worked together in Pleiku, one hell of a good man. He is commanding a neighboring A Detachment, A-239 Luong Son Special Forces Camp, and doing a good job under difficult circumstances.

Captain Jim Richie is a good friend. He commanded A-235 Nhon Co Special Forces Camp before he moved up to the B Team at Buon Ma Thuot. Good southern boy with excellent leadership qualities. Soft spoken and knowledgeable, you want him on your side when the shooting begins.

Captains Daniels, Lee Mize, and Jackson are all great guys and enjoying success at their respective camps.

July 10, 1966 Sure was good to get back to camp, although it was a pleasant change to see the other commanders and all the soldiers at B-23. We had a successful conference. Major Gillette gets his staff to brief us. Then he puts out the mission statement and provides support. We figure out how to execute it using our best resources. He knows the magic of leadership. I really enjoyed getting together with Jackson and Daniels not only to compare notes on running an A Camp but to renew old friendships from our Germany days. While on the return trip with helicopter blades whirling, I read my mail and received a picture of my son, Alexander. Everyone agreed Alexander, was a tiger. I visualize him in a changing world 20 years from now, hopefully no wars. I can see him as an officer, however, just serving a short tour then getting out and going into law. These pleasant thoughts took my mind off the Viet Cong several thousand feet below in the rugged jungle of double and triple canopy vegetation. Then I was reminded by a .51 caliber round piercing the floor by my right foot. We examined the chopper when we got to Tan Rai and that was the only new hole. It was a chance hit by the VC. Fortunately no one got hurt.

Lieutenant Keating is my Civil Affairs and Psychological Operations Officer (CA/PO). He's a leg, (meaning not airborne qualified). He is attached to us from the 41st Civil Affairs/Psychological Operations Company in Saigon. He is a fireball of energy, tall, lanky, intelligent and full of well meaning ideas for projects to help the Yards. He's been a real asset to Tan Rai and an inspiration to all. I give him the ideas and the support, and he gets the job done. He has some good ideas of his own as well. Just to mention a few; building several fish ponds; and harvesting another rice crop for the season. He has an Engineering degree from MIT.

CHAPTER 4 FULRO

Front Unifie' Pour La Liberation Des Races Opprimees
(Unified Front for the Liberation of Oppressed Peoples)
July 11, 1966

Today was a surprisingly progressive day. It took a little while to get started but after a long get organized and quit belly aching lecture to the team everything got rolling. After a few days of absence, progress is evident. The bunkers are almost complete and the toilets, generator shed, and schoolhouse are coming along nicely. The Luc Luong Dac Biet Lieutenant that I put in charge of the school construction has taken ammunition crates and cleverly made benches and desks out of them. Have to give him an A+ for creativity.

Here I need to explain what FULRO is all about.

My interpreter and the LLDB Captain confirmed what I read in a Top Secret, 5th SF Intelligence Summary, before coming to Tan Rai. This is about FULRO and what happened last year and how it effected Tan Rai and the men of this camp.

(The following is paraphrased from after action reports)

The Montagnards revolted from Special Forces' camps in Buon Ma Thuot and the surrounding provincial area. Buon Ma Thuot is a Vietnamese-populated city, but traditionally the Montagnard capital. The Vietnamese contemptuously regard the Montagnards as inferior but dangerous. I've noticed that General Vinh Loc, II Corps commander, is very cautious with the Montagnards. The Vietnamese call them 'Maui' which means savage. Many Vietnamese in Buon Ma Thuot believed that the U.S. had formed a special Montagnard battalion and it was armed with 'two hundred small nuclear weapons.' The Montagnards would not deny this rumor. The Montagnard's attitude toward Vietnamese remained rancorous; one of disrespect and avoidance of the Vietnamese law. Last year the continued mistreatment by Vietnamese authorities heightened the Montagnards grievances.

During the period 19-20 September 1964, the Montagnard strike force represented by components of five CIDG camps took matters into their own hands. The three companies of Mnong and Rhade Montagnards at Bon Sar Pa killed eleven LLDB soldiers in the camp, held the American commander and his Detachment A-311A hostage, and moved northeast on trucks to seize the Buon Ma Thuot radio Station and a key bridge. The radio station was rendered inoperable when the station manager removed certain parts.

Five companies of Rhade and Jarai Montagnards at Ban Don bound their LLDB advisors with rope, initially locked up the Americans of Detachment A-75, and moved southeast toward Buon Ma Thuot. Using trucks, three battalions of Montagnards closed in on the Darlac provincial capital of Buon Ma Thuot. They came from three directions by 0100 hours on 20 September.

Three companies of Mnong Montagnards at Bu Prang slaughtered fifteen Vietnamese strike force leaders and another nineteen Self-Defense Corps soldiers at a nearby outpost and restricted the Detachment A-311B to the camp.

The commander of Detachment A-312 at Buon Brieng had persuaded the 715 Rhade Montagnards stationed there not to follow through with their rebellious intentions. As a result, the Montagnard 'national' flag was not hoisted over the compound as it was at other camps. This was later seen as the critical move that saved Buon Ma Thuot from Montagnard occupation, because it left Highway 14 open from the north. Buon Brieng is where the initial group of Montagnards were recruited for the beginning of Camp Tan Rai because of family ties. I continue to recruit from there.

The 23d ARVN Division and Montagnard troops faced each other uneasily outside Buon Ma Thuot on Sunday, 20 September 1964. That afternoon the detachment commander convinced the Ban Don Strikers to return to camp and escorted the Yards back. There was only one clash at a Buon Mi Ga Montagnard force roadblock, which occurred at 2100 hours and caused ten strike force casualties.

The Bon Sar Pa force was considered the most dangerous, since it had several hundred Vietnamese hostages from its takeover of a district capital on the original march toward Buon Ma Thuot. A colonel arrived to negotiate the prisoner release. At first everything went well, but then the two American Colonels boldly cut the strands binding Lieutenant Chu (the only surviving LLDB prisoner from the Bon Sar Pa Camp) and speeded him onto a waiting helicopter. The Montagnards were infuriated and held both colonels hostage during the night of September 21st and 22nd, 1964.

Although the revolt was quickly ended, the Vietnamese government was forced reluctantly to sit down and discuss Montagnard demands. An ARVN officer of Rhade descent was installed as the camp commander of Ban Don, the last camp to pull down its rebel flag. This officer commanded Tan Rai for a short period while Dai Uy Minh was on leave. The officer was strong, professional, tall and well built and commanded respect. He carried himself with dignity and professionalism approaching charismatic. I was impressed. Rhade ARVN officers were also selected to command Camps Buon Brieng and Buon Mi Ga. By the middle of October, the Montagnard leaders held a congress to present their conditions. Foremost was their desire for a 50,000-man army led by Montagnards and trained exclusively by Special Forces without MAAG (Military Assistance Advisory Group) interference. Before the Saigon regime could respond to the long Montagnard list of demands, the central highlands were deluged by unusually heavy rainstorms during late October and early November. Communications and transportation were completely disrupted.

I continued to question my interpreter who continued to verify what I had read in the Intelligence report. The Vietnamese finally instituted only a few token changes in their governing policies toward the Montagnards. The revolt had merely brought CIDG problems under sharp criticism. MACV was upset that the Montagnards devoted their loyalties to the Special Forces sponsors of the program and not the Saigon government.

I read later in the B team documents, as a final postscript to the 1964 Montagnard revolt, all camps involved were shut down within a year. This was probably due to the perceived threat to the Vietnamese Government. Bon Sar Pa was the first to go, closed down on 1 November 1964. Ban Don was closed out on the first day of the New Year, and Bu Prang followed on 15 January 1965. Later this year 1966 Tan Rai conducted operations at Ban Don. Buon Mi Ga was ordered abandoned on 28 April 1965. I was in Germany at that time just thinking about going to Vietnam and thinking more about my family and pregnant wife. Months later the Vietnamese suddenly declared Buon Brieng to be heavily infiltrated by dissident Montagnards sympathetic to the Rhade independence movement in other words; FULRO. The Yards from Buon Brieng were recruited to start this camp at Tan Rai, along with three of the Special Forces team members who started the camp in 1965. There were also Rhade tribesmen there but mostly K'ho. I am continuing to hire the K'ho tribesmen, as they are more available and easier to recruit because of word of mouth. They are loyal and excellent fighters.

I have ambivalent feelings about the FULRO movement. On one hand I believe in one government and on the other I believe in treating people equally. For some reason those two concepts collide here.

In his book, Colonel Jerry Sage, my commander in Germany, changed the team concept to individual replacements during this time frame. In other words instead of six month team rotation out of Okinawa now it was a one year commitment and individually assigned to the camp where needed.

July 13, 1966 Busy day today at 1400 hours there were two airplanes circling over camp, waiting to land while a helicopter was landing. One was a psychological operations airplane, with a loud speaker. The other was a reconnaissance airplane covering an operation I had going on North of camp. The chopper brought in visitors. I received a radio call from Sergeant Bob "Bull" Durham, whom I put in charge of the operation. He said the rear of his column was ambushed and he had a wounded Striker. By accidental luck I fortuitously sent the chopper to take him to Bao Loc. Charley is playing it smart. He snipes at the rear element and runs.

July 14, 1966 Tonight I was listening to the ARVN operation on the radio. They fight differently. They had a Viet Cong company advancing toward them. They called for overhead cover, flare ships and everything. It was getting dark. The ARVN unit was battalion size. They wouldn't have to worry about a small VC Company. However I guess when you have been fighting for 45 years (Chinese, Japanese, French, NVA) there is not much to gain knowing the probable outcome. I said to my men, "It would be time to set out the claymores and bed down, rather than waste all that energy getting lights overhead. Save the energy for a fight." I prefer to fight while taking advantage of the dark. That's the way I was trained in Ranger school. When you put the illumination up you expose yourself also. The end result was that ARVN had several of their own killed and wounded with no VC head count.

July 15, 1966 A Warrant Officer dumped our food supply on the runway today damaging 80% of it. In his haste, he made waste. He tried to off load too quickly from the Caribou CV-2 or C-7 aircraft. I guess he didn't want to wait around and get mortared. It was a bad scene in front of my Strikers. I was mad. The incident destroyed rapport with the Yards that we had been building.

CHAPTER 5 SUPPORTING A VILLAGE

July 16, 1966 This was a joyous and happy day for Tan Rai. They have never had a school and today the Dai Uy gave them a school. At 0800 hours I drove into the village with my entourage; my counterpart, Dai Uy, Tuai Ta, Master Sergeant Samualson, Lieutenant Keating, and Lieutenant Chester T. Jones, my executive officer. When driving into the village area, the school door flung open and half the children rushed us in glee. It was the moment for which they had been waiting. We rustled them back in their seats and commenced with the opening ceremony. I said a few words and presented the symbolic key to my acting counterpart, a Montagnard Dai Uy. He presented the key to the two Catholic Nun Teachers. They were overjoyed to have their own school. The children were overwhelmed at the excitement and many pictures were taken, unfortunately only a few turned out. It was really a remarkable achievement and all of my team members were proud to be responsible for such a milestone in the history of Tan Rai. Killing VC is not the only way to win a war. Developing these young minds is just as important. Fifteen years from now with their minds developed, they won't want to fight a war but build a country. We are educating the leaders of the 80's and 90's. More accomplishments like this and we are on our way to winning the war. Besides, we'll get plenty of information for our intelligence net from the children, serendipitously. Of course I did not discuss intelligence gathering with the priest and my counterpart. That is between my intelligence sergeant and the one Catholic Nun we recruited.

The village chief of a near village marched 30 of his children up to the school when he heard about the school we built. I promised him with his help I would build him a school. He was overjoyed and agreed to do all the work. I venture to say in a few short weeks we'll have one built for him as well. That means more intelligence gathering opportunities about the activities around his village. It is surprising what these youngsters will tell you in perfect candor. Building a school is really a self-help program. We provide the materials or make them available on the economy and the villagers build under our supervision. Sounds easy huh? Keep in mind their primitive and crude tools and non-technical skill level. It has to be this way because if we Americans build something, the VC will destroy it. If the people build it the VC would be foolish to destroy it.

In 1998 I saw the school in modern times with no less than 2000 students. I did not tell anyone that I started the school. The communist might have made an issue of it and cut my vacation short.

July 17, 1966 An empty C-123 landed today to pick up my Strikers. I will send a company on an operation with the 1st Cavalry Division tomorrow. I directed Chet Jones, who is in charge of the operation, to return with VC weapons. He says he's not coming back unless he does. He sure has a lot of esprit-de-corps and is a fine gentleman. His skill is to come up with the unbelievable and innovative effective ways of achieving the goals with resources available. The morale is very high. I cross my fingers and pray for a successful operation. It will mean a lot. I can't afford to lose any of my Americans. I would suffer greatly if I lost one because we are so few and very close. May God protect them. They will be fighting NVA where they are going. The NVA are professional troops and can really do damage if they engage first. If my company gets attacked I hope air support is available.

Hey, I found out today I have several college students working for me, and they are Montagnards. They will go back to school in September. They are merely summer mercenaries. They seem to do a good job. I figure they'll do a lot for the war effort when they get back to school and tell their buddies about how well they were treated at Tan Rai. I bet we'll have a lot of walk-in recruits. We get about 30 recruits a month as it is. When the Montagnard recruits arrived at camp they wore nothing more than red and black loincloths and carried crude spears and crossbows.

I have over 500 trained soldiers now and growing. My objective is to build to about 700 or 800 well-trained Strikers in order to conduct effective company sized operations. In other words to do a job on Charley.

July 18, 1966 The C-123 Airplane got stuck on the airstrip in the heavy sticky clay like mud. The wheels were buried in about two and a half feet of mud. It just came to a gradual smothered halt and no matter how much he cranked the props, it wouldn't budge. I'll get the bulldozer to pull it out in a few days when the ground dries out.

July 19, 1966 Building a Force

Got Company A off today for their operation. It took four CV-2 lifts. They're going to Ban Don, close to Cambodia. Gave away the PPSH 41 machine gun to Captain Doyle for food. Colonel Francis J. "Blackjack" Kelly, the commander of the 5th Special Forces Group, is coming soon to Tan Rai. When we hear his name we know he is out to relieve someone or put on a blood stripe (A blood stripe is rank just taken from a reduced soldier). The word was that he relieved two A detachment commanders already today.

It is raining every day now. The monsoon is here. Raindrops pound incessantly on you permeating to the bone. It is impossible to stay dry and warm. Green mold grows on clothing and equipment. All efforts go toward keeping warm, healthy and productive. The camp is always muddy and wet. The boot sucking mud is everywhere. Every person is wet to the bone, and has an eerie white eggshell look along with wrinkled fingers that look like mushrooms.

It seems the wet weather brings on lethargic behavior and depression. Depression is an emotion I am acutely aware of and can see it in the men. The men have shorter tempers and seem more depressed so I have to brag on the little accomplishments and listen intently and empathetically. Often the subject is broken hearts. Passive listening is not enough. You have to strike the right cord to get them to talk. Listen to their emotions, not just the content. But talk they must, if not they do crazy things, like slit girl's throats, as one did in DaLat the other day. He didn't kill her, but scared the hell out of her. It was just a superficial wound and no real damage. I got a call from the Province Chief on that one. The human condition certainly changes when one is cold, wet and miserable. First, one is physically more lethargic, secondly, one seems emotionally more irascible and thirdly, pride of character dwindles away and the animal takes over the intellect. As long as I am aware of the possibility of depression and fight it myself, we will survive in a positive progressive way. If I get depressed, the whole camp gets depressed. I won't let that happen.

July 20, 1966 Chung Uy Minh returned from leave today and the Montagnard Dai Uy, who was my acting counterpart, went back to Buon Ma Thuot. The Montagnard Dai Uy is one of a very few Montagnards who have attained the rank of Captain. Lieutenant Minh is preoccupied with his difficulties and tends to prefer staying in his own thoughts instead of taking action. Too much stress causes him to become excessively indecisive reticent and recalcitrant all at the same time. He can be caring toward his family, but generally has that perceived academy officer stand off appearance and is not close to his men. He does not disclose anything about his personal life. He wants to be accepted but hesitates to present negative information about himself. It rained all day today. Tan Rai is slowing down construction as a result of wetness. Everyone worked in the rain with little progress.

I was reading an old area assessment of Tan Rai and looking at overlays. It seems the VC were more active in those days around Tan Rai. Funny thing, they used the exact same routes three years ago as they use today. They stick to the boundaries, especially between provinces and districts and stay outside Artillery range. There are fewer VC in number now. There are only 2,500 in the province of Lam Dong. Three years ago there were twice as many. Their unit designations have stayed the same. Albeit, I feel an increase of VC in my bones. Intuitively, I feel units are infiltrating in and something unusual is about to happen.

July 21, 1966 Operation

This is an entirely different feeling than in camp. This is nature at its purest. The predawn smells of wet foliage and rotting humus awakens in you a sense of purpose with nature. Moist earth hangs heavily in the air. The sky above the single canopy jungle glows with the first hints of dawn as the jungle comes to life.

After lacing up my boots, I stood and stretched, listening for unusual sounds. Except for the periodic sounds of insects, birds, and the faint rustling of monkeys, everything seemed normal. I did a few toe touches to loosen my cramped back muscles and get my juices flowing. Sleeping in a hammock limits you to one position...curved on your back, which is good because you are at the ready. I opened a package of lightweight; dehydrated Vietnamese rations and buried the olive-drab plastic paper. I was humorously reminded of my fraternity brother who, after graduation, helped his father in his C-Ration operation at Blue Star Foods where they made perfectly good money on perfectly normal chickens that they crammed into the C ration cans to be eaten by soldiers at base camp. The canned version is too heavy for my type of operations. We have to travel light and besides I believe in eating the same food my troops eat.

I glanced to my left and recognized the silhouette of Bac Xi Vanhorne rolling out of his hammock. With a perpetual smile on his baby face and an optimistic, "Morning Dai Uy,"

To the Yards he is affectionately known as Bac Xi, which means Doctor.

"My feet look like Mushrooms we used to find along the Mississippi River, in Crystal City Missouri." I commented.

Since the Viet Cong usually attacked at first light, we made it a practice to have everyone up and ready to move before dawn. Bending over beside my ruck, I opened the side pocket and removed a toothbrush and toothpaste. A splash of water on my face and the sweet smell of Colgate was a real treat. Even though my body was covered with layers of dried sweat, mosquito repellent, and jungle grime from the previous days, this morning ritual somehow made me feel clean.

Larry squatted beside the PRC-25 radio and proceeded with the radio check.

"Is our primary frequency still 35.5?"

"Yeah," with a quick glance to the pad perpetually strapped around my neck. The jungle was still dominated by slate grays when Larry picked up the handset and whispered into the mouthpiece.

"Sierra Five, this is Tiger Six Alpha, commo check, over." That transmission suddenly seemed to be the conduit of life.

"Tiger Six Alpha, this is Sierra Five, five by, over," Lieutenant Jones responded from his position inside our perimeter.

"Roger, Sierra Five, I hear you same. Out."

When Larry completed the morning radio check we finished packing our rucks.

"We'd better change that battery, Sir."

"I agree Larry."

K'Gee had the typical Yard build muscular and sinewy; a compressed little man with a copper-brown tint who stood about chest-high.

K'Gee had a friendly face with a disarming smile which concealed a fierce hatred for the Vietnamese and intense loyalty to Americans and his men. During off-duty hours he is a very easygoing person who has a fatherly relationship with the younger Yards in the Battalion. During operations he transforms into a hardened warrior who tolerates nothing less than instant, willing obedience from his men. He knows that discipline is one of the keys to survival. A unit that fights as individuals won't last long, but a unit that fights as one team can slug it out with anyone. On more than one occasion I saw him sink his boot in subordinate's rear end. But he never really hurt any of his men, just scared the hell out of them. His troops fear him more than the VC but revere him unquestionably.

As the jungle unfolded ahead of us its beauty and variety overwhelmed me. Towering brown-black trees supported a canopy of green foliage like the four-story pillars of an ancient temple. In the lower levels of the canopy, gnarled vines twisted off in all directions or dangled like limp tentacles from branches overhead. Occasionally, vines ensnared the trunks of trees as if struggling to strangle them in some quiet death grip. At the lower levels, the jungle was clotted with lush foliage. Here and there stood stands of bamboo clumped together like bundles of lime-green poles and enormous broad leaves and palm fronds. The smell of mold, mildew, and decaying vegetation accented the air. Tangled vines, vegetation, ferns and moss were wet and dripping from the perpetual humidity. Everything seemed to sweat in the dawn.

"Are you up tight?" Larry asked in a concerned voice. We returned to welcome arms at the camp. It is rewarding to return from a successful operation.

July 22, 1966 It rained all night and the wind almost blew my tent down. We're all above ground in tents but building underground shelters. The first task was to get the ammunitions bunker below ground level.

We received credible intelligence from the Company we sent out a few days ago. They captured documents.

July 23, 1966 Luong Son was mortared tonight, one friendly killed and forty-five wounded. They will be med-evac'd in a CV-2. I feel bad for Don Sweigart; all that trouble. Last I remember of him he was so enthusiastic about all the good happenings in his camp. C'est La Vie... C'est La Gverre", (such is life...such is war). It's raining hard now. It will probably rain all through the night as the monsoon season continues. Tan Rai is on a bald hill mass pulsating with energy and poised for action, ready for something to happen in spite of the muddy surface. Friendships and respect are forged on operations. The crucible of combat would be a good phrase here. When one is under fire with a fellow Special Forces buddy and the fear of God screams across our faces just inches apart there is a bond of intimacy that will last forever. I've read about this and now I know. Specialist Eugene Tafoya is one of the survivors, someone who, through luck, skill or whiley skills, has managed to stay alive. He is an infantryman with communications competencies acting in the position of Demolitionist departing Vietnam 9 December 1966. Knowing him, he will likely extend. He stares through a ruddy face with penetrating blue eyes. His youth must have been in the barrio fighting for his life and survival. He was the defensive tackle on the football team. Gene is the kind of person whom others might describe as eccentric. He won't impress you with his friendliness and may even frighten you with his manner. I can always count on him for results on operations but cringe when I allow him to go to Dalat and Saigon.

SECTION THREE: OPERATIONS

CHAPTER 6 SMALL UNIT OPERATIONS

July 24, 1966 Just checked the defenses around camp. It's early 0515 hours. It's raining as usual and the night is pitch black. Charley could attack us today. We don't have a reaction force out and I found out my ambushes are not as effective as I was led to believe. I understand that three of the squads, instead of manning sites, went to the local tavern and drank all night. That is what happens when we Americans are not on operations with them. I will take their money away, for starters. The ambushes are important because as a small force we want to select the time, place, and circumstances of all contact with the enemy. As guerrillas we want to initiate contact, ideally, only when we have thoroughly calculated the odds and are fairly certain we can win. Then I hear that the village chief has a drinking party at 0900 hours this morning. I have not figured that one out yet; some sort of celebration? What are we celebrating? Or is it their way of fighting depression, by getting drunk? That's not very considerate of me because the truth is the only way they use drugs or alcohol is in a spiritual way. I reckon that justifies it. Maybe evil spirits are lurking about? There seems to be a trend toward drinking and drunkenness when nothing else is happening.

The village elders were sacrificing the remainder of the buffalo herd because of one buffalo dying. My Team Executive Officer put a halt to that. He convinced them that if we immunized the rest of the herd no more would die. This was not an easy task in view of their animalism and spirit beliefs.

July 25, 1966 It is now 0200 hours and I Just got off guard. The high winds almost blew our tents over again. The rains are constant. It is a bitter chilling cold when we are not used to it and are not clothed for it. I showed movies to the Strikers last night. We use an 8-millimeter projector driven by a small generator. When I started the film it was backward. So we ran it backward and laughed all the way through the movie. The Yards have difficulty when we talk rapidly anyway. They thoroughly enjoyed it.

Later in the day at the village I gave the kids a ride in my jeep and, as usual, gave them candy. The school that we built for the village people continues to be a success. Gathering of intelligence is easier now that we have the children's input. We had a formation and ceremony for the opening of the American latrine. Lieutenant Keating checked it out and officially broke the seal. We named it "No Mo' Waiting", in honor of Sergeant First Class Waits who built it. The Montagnard carpenters put the stool on backwards, not having seen one before.

July 26, 1966 We showed "Gun smoke" tonight, this time in the forward mode. The Yards seemed to enjoy it even more.

I started lifting weights last night in addition to my modified physical fitness routine. I cannot run five miles around here so I run in place. I also gave Judo classes to my Strikers. They think that is the greatest. It's "Poc" time now. The rains are beating down as they did all night so I can't think of a better reason to lie down and take a nap. I took some books down to the school today. I just wrote the Monthly Operations Summary (MOPSUM). This afternoon I will write awards for my soldiers.

After Guard duty from 2200 to 2400 I played poker with the night owls.

July 27, 1966 I won $10. This rainy season is getting to be a drag. It presents many problems: slows aircraft, slows construction, hampers morale and more importantly, it cuts down on combat operations. But I guess the VC have the same problems. Can you imagine sitting out there in the jungle under a poncho and a coolie cap? Or in a damp tunnel? The sun poked through the clouds briefly today. It was literally a site for sore eyes.

July 28, 1966 MY SON, ALEXANDER's, FIRST BIRTHDAY!

To my son Alexander:

They say every generation has its War. I had mine early in my career. It's trite, but I hope you, Alexander, won't have yours. I know if there is one, you will be the type of man who will be in the middle of it. I'd like to think you will be above that and rather than having a rifle and grenade, you will be dictating policies. My advice to you Alexander is be honest and stay ahead of the power curve. You have the latent potential from your mom.

July 29, 1966 This was indeed a long day. At 0430 hours I received a call telling me a General and several Colonels were coming here at 0900 hours. We got ready for them. The helicopter got lost and the General disembarked at Bao Loc. However, Lt. Colonel William A. Patch, Colonel Phong, Major Bud Gillette and Major John S. (Jack) Kistler made it in. I really respect these men. They understand what is going on and are very supportive. They were impressed with the progress and our intelligence gathering. I must admit everything went well. My counter-part and I dazzled them with a briefing on the improvements and operations. We showed all camp progress, operations, village progress, the school, and the intelligence net. They could not believe the progress Camp Tan Rai has made. We presented Colonel Patch with a plaque. He is leaving soon. I hate to see him go. He understands this kind of warfare more than anyone in II Corps. I wish the best for him. He is certainly destined to become a General officer.

My Strikers returned from the combat operation today. They were very successful. They netted several VC KIA and captured a lot of supplies without taking casualties. Everything is going great, so great I am afraid that something catastrophic is going to happen. I received my week's mail today also. That made me very happy. I had to start the day off though chewing everyone's ass because of a few small tasks my people failed to do. I had to remind them of their responsibilities. After that everything was up tight.

July 31, 1966 The pay officer flew in and a Lieutenant Colonel Fernandez was along for a visit. Captain Leonardo C. Thomas, the B-23 Personnel Officer, says this camp has progressed more in the past 30 days then any camp in Vietnam. I was proud to hear that.

Aug 1, 1966 **Official Flag Raising Ceremony**

All LLDB (Vietnamese Special Forces) and USSF (United States Special Forces) stood in front of the troops and the flag was raised for the first time at this camp. Everyone saluted with pride. My counterpart and I gave a motivational speech then we got on with the day's chores.

Aug. 2, 1966 Flew to Bao Loc to coordinate combat operations and talk to the Province Chief. On the return trip I flew the L-19 for about an hour, looking for VC. Found a few new VC shelters. God gave man the most important element for human happiness, and that is- individuality. That is the first thing man will trade for acceptance, a trait that is not in the realm of survival. I was inspired to think this today flying around and realizing how free and independent I am as the commander of this camp, and comparing myself to others with whom I come in contact. This is the best A Camp in Vietnam and because we are showing progress we are left alone to create our own individuality. The men feel proud of their accomplishments.

Aug. 3, 1966 All sorts of commotion but no fatalities. One of my companies made contact with Charley today. We just happened to have two airplanes on our airstrip. The pilots were having dinner with us so Jones and I flew up to look for the VC squad or platoon. Didn't spot anything. I was firing an M-79 grenade launcher and the pilot, the "chief," was firing an M-60 machine gun that he mounted on his left wing. I flew awhile and almost crashed into a mountain. The chief pulled it up for me just in time.

Just about a half-hour ago I heard a muffed shot. It was one Striker shooting another. I don't know yet if it was an accident or deliberate. He took the round just below the navel almost in the groin. It came out the buttocks. I called the light aircraft L-19 down and the wounded Striker should be in Bao Loc now under medical treatment. I sure hope that we do not lose him. "Bac Xi" gave him morphine. It's "poc" time. I'll sleep for an hour. I hope no one wakes me.

Earlier today I sent a road clearing operation out and later I drove down to Mnrong Sekang and took medicine and propaganda leaflets there. In the village my CA/PO (Civil Affairs and Psychological Operations) Officer, Lieutenant Keating, was taking Polaroid pictures. The Yards looked in disbelief at the instant results. They think the picture is attached to their spirit. We use the photos for intelligence purposes. I am expecting a battalion of ARVN to stage out of here this afternoon.

It is now 1830 hours. The ARVN battalion arrived and is outside our perimeter now. I invited the officers to sit at our dinner table this evening. They commented that we lived well. Tomorrow they kick off their operation. I'm sending a small force to guide them and to return to camp a different route, checking out a VC suspected area. That is a clever way of getting into Charlie's territory without being detected. I would venture to say my reconnaissance element comes up with more than the ARVN battalion does. We'll see.

Aug. 4, 1966 Was picked up today by Major Gillette to attend the A-Team leaders meeting at Buon Ma Thuot. He said,

"Ray, you have the Model A camp of II Corps now. I guess you know that?"

I shrugged as if to say yes, but inwardly I welled up with pride to hear it for the first time and from my commander whom I respect so much.

Went to two A Detachments; Don Sweigart's A-239 Luong Son where the flat, sandy terrain was in stark contrast to the verdant green jungles of Tan Rai. Then to Lee Mize's camp Dong Ba Tin. After that we flew to the B Detachment at Buon Ma Thuot. I am observing that men live up to or down according to your expectations of them. Therefore I must always articulate high expectations, for if I settle for less, I get less.

Aug. 6, 1966 Meeting all day today. Getting a lot done- All those things that have to be coordinated which no one does for you while you are out in the sticks. B Team party tonight. That means to the club to meet new people, and tell war stories.

Aug. 8, 1966 Still waiting for aircraft. I wrote a letter of commendation for one of my soldiers and generally coordinated supply and operational activities.

Aug.10, 1966 Returned to Tan Rai with the L-19 pilot, Mr. Thomas, today. He is one great pilot and selfless in his duty ethic.

Aug. 11, 1966 It's now 0900 hours, Colonel 'Blackjack' Francis J. Kelly is expected here today.

It's now 1600 hours. He came, he saw, he liked, and he left. Now we wait for the word to come down officially. Did he really like what we were doing or will there be changes? One always wonders; Colonel Kelly is notorious for relieving commanders on the spot. Prior to visiting our camp he relieved two people. He relieves at one camp and promotes at another. I guess today was promotion for us. I personally don't see anything wrong with his method. It is firm, consistent and decisive. But it is not my style.

Aug. 12, 1966 Sent two Americans to the hospital with Malaria. Received a new man. SSG Robert L. Clark, Communications Sergeant, appears self assured and confident and quite capable. After talking with him a bit it appears he is people oriented and relationships are likely to be of primary importance to Bob. He prefers physical and intellectual risks to emotional ones. He has a strong instinct in judging people. Totally loyal and reliable he can be trusted to make split second decisions based on good values. His standards tend to be so stringent that most people fall short of meeting his requirements. I'm sure when Bob is under pressure; he will perform in a positive way.

Went to the village to visit the school. Instructed and taught children to sing "Amen."

The Striker that got shot last week died. The Striker who shot him goes on with normal duty.

I've got about 30 AWOLS. I received a report that the VC are going to attack this camp and are working on an attack plan using a *sandtable this very moment. They keep saying that. I wish the hell they would try it with a battalion. We would clean house.

*Note: Sandtable is a display about 1 meter by 1 meter displaying using dirt or sand the exact replica of camp Tan Rai.

Aug. 13, 1966 While General Westmoreland meets with President Johnson at the LBJ ranch today and tomorrow, we are getting all our supplies in from airlifts.

Everything is going real fine. The only problem is that there are not enough hours in a day. We work at least twelve to sixteen hours but that's still not enough.

Hooray! I received three wonderfully welcomed letters from Heidi. She is undoubtedly the best thing that ever happened to me. She can transmit emotion via a single letter. I hope to God she likes the USA when we eventually get stationed there.

Aug. 14, 1966 Its 0100 hours and I am on guard. I just checked an intelligence source and found the VC are setting up an ambush in the exact spot that we zapped one not long ago. I suppose they are trying to even up the score, or replace a bad spirit with a good one. On the other hand, it may not be as simple as that. They may be manning an outpost or changing their tactics. At any rate I do not think they want us up north. There must be something happening north of the ambush, maybe a meeting or visit by an NVA VIP?

We're getting ready for the official camp opening on August 15th, tomorrow. I expect that's a good time to get hit by the VC if they ever intend to do so. I think that they will mortar us. We shall see. Everyone is getting in the preparatory mode for the ceremony. The village chief has three fancy traditional wooden poles. He is also breaking out 10 jugs of Nam Pai (rice wine). I had a buffalo flown in today for the ceremony so they don't have to take from their own herd. The battalion commander will get his people to parade around in costumes and kill the buffalo in their traditional brutal, but spiritual, way. The LLDB are sprucing up the place with a cosmetic facelift. The troops are working hard at various projects. There is an energy level here that goes unsurpassed.

HELPING THOSE THAT HELP THEMSELVES

It is 1800 hours and I just returned from a CA/PO medical patrol in the village of Mnrong Sekang. Upon entering the village we announced on the loud speaker that we had a doctor and medical supplies. We instructed the villagers to assemble at the town hall, actually it was the village chief's house. The thatched house was filled with smoke, had a dirt floor, and bamboo siding. We gave red pills for backaches, green for stomachaches and yellow ones for headaches. My "doctor" obviously fixed up the ones that were really sick. We check their hands to see if they have been carrying weapons by using a heat/metal-detecting device. We incarcerated two VC suspects. We gave away clothing to win some hearts and minds. The clothes came from Crystal City, Missouri. My high school classmates came through. The village chief opened a new jug of Nam Pai for us in thanks and celebration.

CHAPTER 7 CAMP TAN RAI OPENING CEREMONY

August 15, 1966 The Province Chief and Senior Sector Advisor both Colonels arrived about 1030 hours at which time I asked them to cut the ceremonial ribbon, and officially open TAN RAI A-232. After that came the flag raising, speeches, skit, sacrificing the buffalo, drinking rice wine and eating an abundance of delicious food. The skit was about a VC killing the wrong person. Everyone laughed hysterically. After the VIP's left, the village chief invited Sergeant Major Samualson and I to pray with him. I felt like an observer, detached, as we stood by the stake while they killed the buffalo and held the food, clasped our hands and then they looked down at the sacrificial chicken and buffalo and prayed. The buffalo blood and small pieces of meat were inserted by the chief at various places on the pole while internal organs were thrown to the wind as a display of reverence. Finally, we were offered to eat raw red meat. It was raw buffalo liver, not too bad. We drank newly uncorked rice wine. Uncorked in the sense that a large mud and grass cap is removed from the large vase. In my mind I thought it tastes like the urine of a buffalo served inside it's spleen truthfully it was tolerable. Then we accepted a symbol of rice and eggs and presented meat to the subordinate village chiefs. I think I will give the troops a holiday tomorrow in the spirit of the celebration. It was another enduring day as we learned more about the spirits lurking over Tan Rai.

August 16, 1966 Three CV-2's flew in with supplies. It was a day to receive and stock-up supplies, plan operations and catch up on letter writing.

Aug. 17, 1966 Intelligence sources say there were a few VC just outside camp this evening so we pumped out a few mortar rounds on suspected positions. I had to relieve a company commander due to his incompetence. The Tui Ta, LLDB executive officer, is in command of the camp now that Thung Uy Minh is gone for a few days. I wonder where he goes, when he goes, and what he does? He is so secretive.

Just before he left we had a discussion on when we were born. I told him I was born in 1938. He said that was the year of the Tiger. I asked "What does that mean?" He proceeded to tell me. "Capable of great love." However, I have a tendency to get carried away and be stubborn about what I think is right. I don't know if he was making that up because he does not like me horning in on his graft operations. He went on to say I would be an excellent boss, explorer or matador. He said Marco Polo and Mary Queen of Scots were born in the year of the tiger.

I ask him when he was born. He said, the way you occidentals look at it, it is in 1941 that is the year of the Snake. I said go on. He said the person born of this sign is wise and romantic and deep thinking. The snake is most content as a teacher, philosopher or a fortuneteller. He said Charles Darwin was born in the year of the Snake.

Heidi writes that our friend from Germany, Major McNamara, was killed. I thought I read that in the Army Times.

Aug. 18, 1966 A Fellow SF Commander and Good Friend is Killed In Action. What a travesty, I lost a real friend, Captain Wells Cunningham. Major Gillette flew in today just to relay the news to me. He knew Wells and I were good friends. Wells and two other Americans and a company of Montagnards got wiped out up near the Cambodian border outside his A Camp, Duc Co yesterday. That's the camp to which I was almost assigned but Colonel William Patch did not give it to me because I was married and Wells was a bachelor. Wells and I both knew, the Commander, whomever it would be, would get killed, in fact Wells would tell me about it and later write me about it. I pulled out a letter that Wells had written back in April. (See Appendix 3)

Years later I met the Survivor Assistance Officer, LTC Joe McDonnell.

I asked Joe, "Was it true about the Mercedes and the money clause in the Will?"

He said, "50-50, the Will had to be honored but Wells was not buried in his Mercedes."

I conjured up an inward smile and thought that old fox, he knew all along but still wanted to start a rumor about his idea of being buried in his black Mercedes. I gained more respect for my fallen brother, not less.

I read on the VN Wall in Washington DC in 1981, 15 years later; Wells Eldon Cunningham, Saint Joseph Missouri KIA August 17, 1966 born November 19th 1939, Captain, Armor, Located at 10E-15Line.

This was another crisis day at Tan Rai. Higher headquarters was calling on the Collins single side band radio, trying to find out what was going on. I had one company in formation when the commander informed me that they were quitting. Over 100 men quitting. I could not believe my ears. This threat has high visibility especially because of FULRO (Autonomous movement of the Montagnards) activity in this area. These Yards in particular are perceived to be a threat by the Vietnamese leadership. In fact, some of these 'Yards' came from Colonel Eber Hon's battalion at Bon Brieng. The II Corps Commander, General Vinh Loc, feels threatened by the FULRO movement. He fears they could topple his regime.

Standing firm in front of the company, even though my knees were shaking, I told them to turn in their weapons, equipment, and clothing and get out of my camp if they quit. I told them to get their dependents out of my Striker village and move out immediately. They formed up and talked it over, but balked. They said, "Dai Uy We stay."

I was sure happy to hear they were staying. It was a major crisis at our camp and we survived. Command is not easy. It is gratifying, trying, interesting, hard work, and physically and mentally challenging but not easy. It was a turning point in the history of camp Tan Rai. Now the Strikers, LLDB, and Americans know who the commander is — Dai Uy Striler. They cannot bluff. The only thing that worries me now is that the Strikers act afraid of me when I walk around. I don't see their usual smiling faces. They coy, much like a runt dog in a litter. The older custom of not looking a superior in the eye is evident again. Is it because of this crisis? For a while they were looking me in the eye as a friend. Now It's back on the throne again. Oh well, some time leadership is lonely.

Aug. 19, 1966 General Heintges, General Westmoreland's deputy visited us today. He takes a real interest in our camp and was very interesting to talk with. He was here about an hour and a half. I gave him a briefing, showed him the camp and the village of Tan Rai. He enjoyed the tour. I have an intuitive feeling the estimate of VC out there is double what we report. Why would General Heintges visit my camp? What is going on? What does he know that we don't? What is the Vietcong up to? Wrote Heidi a letter today. I tell her everything about the people but not much about the job.

Aug. 20, 1966 Dalat Local Rest and Recuperation (R & R) I flew to the lovely picturesque Provincial city of DaLat today to coordinate with the province chief about recruiting. I was fortunate to see Clyde Sincere, Major Bud Gillette, Logan, Sp4 Robert F. Williams, my Weapons Sergeant, and "Goose" Tatum (Team Sergeant for A 235). DaLat is a resort town high in the mountains of the central highlands. It is seated at 4300 feet elevation and enjoys fresh cool weather year around. It lies in a mountain range where around it tower mountains up to 8000 feet. Everything is peaceful and quiet. The vegetation reminds me of the forest in Gardener Montana, where I worked with the Forest Service during my college summer break.

After three long months I finally got away from the A Camp to relax. My good buddy Wesby came flying into Tan Rai to pick me up. He said I am taking your commander on vacation. DaLat was about 20 minutes flying distance to the East. I had heard it was a beautiful mountain resort for the VC.

We flew East over Bu Dop where I remembered a big firefight and losing K'Gee's brother. It seemed so intense at the time. Now the fighting area seemed so small and insignificant. A chilling calm passed through me as I looked down. Wesby flies at tree top level. He hollered over his shoulder,

"Charley has less time to fire at me at tree top." He is a most prodigious pilot. He and the small aircraft (L-19) seemed to be one as he calmly weaves in and out of the triple canopy jungle subtly. He looked over his shoulder and asked,

"Ray have you ever felt G force?"

" I don't recall" I shouted abruptly, thinking to myself, is it possible in this small plane?

Immediately I heard the acceleration and I saw him pull the stick straight back to his belly button. It seemed as if we were going straight up. Once he got 3,000 feet above the treetops, he shoved the stick forward and kept the acceleration forward, then he climbed again using the forward thrust speed to his advantage. Just at the apex of the climb everything seemed weightless. In fact I saw the cigarette in front of him rise up the window as the harness on my shoulders rose up slightly. I thought momentarily that I should have stayed in camp.

Suddenly we were in the middle of DaLat in a Lambretta and Wesby was taking me to his favorite place. As we walked in I noticed the door was painted green. I thought of the song 'The Green Door' by Jim Lowe. I was soon to find out. It was wall-to-wall beautiful women in their Au Dai dresses.

I found a tour guide to take me to the zoo. Soon we were in a Taxi. It was an old black French Citron. I climbed in the back seat. I remember the reverse doors and the large back seat area. The zoo was out of town about seven miles. As we drove out we came up to a VC tax collection checkpoint on the highway. Two VC were manning it with a machine gun. They had this wooden board painted with something written in Vietnamese, which pivoted upward with a rock on the slight end. I was scared shitless. I only had my .32 caliber pistol. My guide said,

"Get down."

I hugged the floor as if I were a floor mat and we barreled right past at about 20 miles an hour. I pulled my pistol out and trained it on the guide. I don't know why I did that, instinct I guess. They laughed and hollered something as we drove past. I couldn't enjoy myself all day knowing we had to go back through the checkpoint. The taxi waited for us for a few hours as I rode the elephant and walked around the zoo. The drive back was uneventful. We went through the VC check point with the same ease as before. This time when the guide hollered, I heard one of them holler a name back. That puzzled me. Stayed the night in DaLat.

Aug 21,1966 Flew back to Tan Rai today early. The stench of diesel fuel burning the contents of the camp's four-hole crapper reminded me I was home. It's Sunday and not much going on. Mr. Ngiep, a local contractor, came to the camp and offered me a pair of ivory elephant tusk mounted on a teakwood stand. He presumably engraved my name in brass. They stood to my eye level. They must have been seven feet long. I'm sure they were quite valuable.

Mr. Ngiep said,

"They are yours Dai Uy, a gift from me."

"Right! Mr. Ngiep, what do you want for them?"

"Nothing."

He had been trying to get an old hulk of a deuce and a half truck that had been cannibalized and was virtually a striped down chassis. He knew we would never use it. "No thanks, I don't need them."

When I refused his gift he became quite indignant and left. I told him to take the tusks with him. The nerve of that guy! The truck was not mine to give.

Aug 22,1966 CWO Thomas gave me a flying lesson today in the L-19.

Aug 23,1966 Flew to Bao Loc for coordination of up coming operations. Alpha company incarcerated 7 VC suspects, but we could not prove they were VC, except for one, who was obvious, by the information he was carrying. I recruited the VC for my intelligence net and turned them loose. I put a trail man on them.

Sent two people who had confiscated a weapon to my intelligence officer in Bao Loc for questioning. I had the passing thought, "Was their motive to make money or to give the weapon to the VC?

Aug 24,1966 I'll soon be losing 40% of my Americans due to rotation, In-Theater Transfer (ITT), and malaria. When one forgets to take the malaria pill its simple, he gets malaria. It is easy to forget to take the pill. One should take it every seven days. I've been determined to take mine but sometime I miss by a few days when I'm on operations. The female anopheles mosquito bites A-Team commanders just as she does others. That's why I can tolerate the mosquito net, small price to pay. Experienced people are leaving and they are being replaced by good people with no combat experience. I am sure however that everything will continue to run smoothly and effectively. I am still under the assumption that I will go to Hong Kong soon as planned, probably on the first of September. I am anxious to go and relax and buy things and be in a safe area for awhile. What will it be like? When I get back I will have served one half of my tour and a good half at that. Time has flown by and I am sure that considering the job I have cut out for me, time will fly for the next six months.

Aug 25,1966 Flew to Bao Loc today.

Aug 26,1966 Flew to Nha Trang today for coordination and to sign for equipment. I held a dependent alert. Again we lined all families up on the airstrip and counted. All of the dependents after three tries made it to the camp and fighting bunkers in 15 minutes from the village halfway down the runway. That's incredible considering there are over 500 families.

Aug 27,1966 Signed for the equipment and picked up supplies. Ran around with Smitty.

Aug 28,1966 Swam in the South China Sea and dove around a sunken wooden Japanese ship.

Aug 29,1966 I flew to Buon Ma Thuot. Packed to go on leave to Hong Kong.

Aug 30,1966 Flew to Saigon. Stayed at the Special Forces Liaison Office (LNO), coordinated transportation to Hong Kong. Flew on an embassy flight, talked to Buck Ashby.

Aug 31,1966 As I checked in to fly to Hong Kong the Air Force Sergeant said I could not take my M-16 with me. I had not thought about it much until then because I just came from the boonies. I said OK you hold it until I return. He looked stunned but took it. I did not even get his name I was so excited to get on the plane. But I remembered that he had red hair.

HONG KONG R&R
Flew to Hong Kong at 1430 hours, dinner on the plane.
The first person I met there was Mr. Lee. Mr. Lee and his
family of at least nine entrepreneurs purchased
everything I could think of and then some. He brought
his brother to measure me for a suit, took me to buy
diamonds and a Rolex and told me where to tour. His
cousins took me to buy ivory and he showed me around
in a taxi, both car and boat. I rode a Rickshaw for the
first time. It was a blast. Stayed in the Hong Kong
Hilton-very plush, $14 a day. The Money exchange here
fluctuates daily. About 4.75 is the normal rate per US $.
September 1, 1966 Hong Kong
Shopped in China Fleet Club. Toured the New Frontier.
Swam, sat in sauna, rode Rickshaw. It was expensive.
September 2, 1966 We had dinner at the Kowloon
Restaurant with Mr. Lee, an Air Force Colonel and a
Captain. I had shrimp, Peking duck-really delicious. I
enjoyed immensely the Cantonese food. The people here
are really helpful, entrepreneurial, busy and nice to
Americans. Moved to the President hotel on the
Kowloon side. The Hilton is on the Hong Kong side. The
Kowloon side is where all the shopping areas are.
September 3, 1966 Hong Kong
HALF WAY POINT; 182.5 DAYS AND A WAKE UP
This is one of the most industrious cities I've ever been
in. The shops and displays are tremendously plentiful.
One can find just about anything here, even from
communist country origin. One must possess a
certificate of origin if anything from Red China is
purchased.
Hong Kong has a 100 year lease from Red China and has
32 years left on that lease. People speculate, all kinds of
fate, however, as long as Red China can get her products
on the world market why shouldn't she let Hong Kong
maintain its independence? That's the positive outlook.
September 4, 1966 Hong Kong

Purchased a Rolex watch, 2 diamonds, 4 sapphires, brass table setting, an ivory chess set and chop sticks. Seeing so many diamonds in trays upon trays was overwhelming. I had to keep reminding myself of the four C's in buying; Clarity, Cut, Color and Carat. I read the DeBeers book so I would be prepared to purchase.

September 6, 1966 Hong Kong

Peak tour: My last day in Hong Kong I wonder if I spent my time and money properly. The first of the day was getting packed and organizing myself to ensure that I had forgotten nothing. In the evening I took the train to the Peak and purchased fresh fruit and ambled along the sidewalk overlooking Hong Kong and Kowloon about 500 feet above the bay. It was stunning, beautiful and intriguing and pulsating with energy. The lights danced as the traffic coiled around the city like a giant snake.

It was eerie, as I seemed to shift from my intellectual state back to my animal essence as I boarded the plane. I had to psyche myself up again for the war zone. I had to survive so I could return to my family.

September 7, 1966 SAIGON

Flew to Saigon and while on the plane I wondered if my M-16 would be there. Could I recognize the Sergeant to whom I gave it? Maybe he had DEROSED (Date of Estimated Return from Overseas) I found him and he gave it back to me.

The normal Striler luck prevailed on the return trip. I had a stand by ticket; the plane carried 83 passengers. There were 82 booked and I just happened to be the 1st on the stand by list. Saved $91.00 by taking that flight. Also just prior to leaving Hong Kong I made my usual good purchase. I bought a radio for Mr. Johnson which sells for $51.00 I paid $42.00 for it and the plane waited for me while I finished the deal. I then met Ham who works for the C. I. A. He was certainly enjoyable to talk with. I actually talked and listened straight for five hours. That's almost a record for me. The only thing that slowed him down was when the airplane dropped from 20,000 feet to 1,000 feet and pulled a G or two on our frail tired bodies. He sweated somewhat and squirmed but continued the discussion something about the upcoming elections. We were wound up tighter than banjo strings. We were going out with a doctor we met to have a few drinks, but we were told the town was off limits to military personnel because of the election. We agreed that it would be unwise to continue the evening as planned so I went to the Special Forces bar where I joined Captain Merritte H. Wilson whom I knew from Germany and we proceeded to drink and discuss the 10th Special Forces. I went to bed at 0200 hours. I must get up early for the courier flight to Nha Trang.

As I was thinking of the reality of operations that I had to look forward to at Tan Rai, I had to get psyched up for the killing, or else I might do something really stupid on operations and get myself zapped. I fell into a deep sleep totally exhausted.

CHAPTER 8 POLITICS

September 8, 1966 Nha Trang, this place changes faces and perspective almost daily. The officers club, huge and bright, is still catering to the endless flow of transient officers. I knew most of the people. The ones I did not know before in Europe, I've met since I have been here. The town is still off limits due to the anticipation of riots during the national elections.

I was walking into a bar down town while at the door I ran into Captain Rodgers, my ROTC instructor. However it was now MSG (Master Sergeant) Rodgers. Was I shocked? The RIF (reduction in force) caught up with him. He was the best in our opinion. I felt the Army screwed up on that one. It made me realize the green machine was capable of dehumanizing its decisions.

September 9, 1966 I saw a lot of crop dusters at the airport. There seems to be an increase in aerial crop-destruction in Viet Cong held territory to clear out areas of perceived travel. I wonder how effective it is and if it could cause health problems?

Good to get back to see the old gang but there were many new faces staring at me. Many had rotated and fresh new recruits were there eager and yet unscathed by the war. As I came into the B-team, I saw the staff all spit shined giving a VIP briefing to a visiting General. It appeared glamorous and impressive but lacking and wanting of real substance especially that which happens at the A Detachment level. I felt like interrupting and telling them what was really going on at the A camp but I bit my tongue and moved on.

September 10, 1966 One of my squads walked into an ambush today at Tan Rai. Two Strikers were evacuated to this location at Buon Ma Thuot. They were seriously wounded, one in the stomach the other in the head. My ex-doctor now stationed here at Buon Ma Thuot said half sarcastically and matter of factly,
"Looks like someone shot them."
His unexpected underpinning dry sarcasm seemed to relieve my anxiety. But I could not get my mind off my two wounded Strikers. I wonder which two; did I know them personally? Doc was previously at Tan Rai; unfortunately I had to give him up to higher headquarters. We sure miss him. We visited the wounded Strikers. They recognized both of us, but I barely recognized them.
September 11, 1966 Tan Rai Election Day; Political Unrest
As I drove to the Buon Ma Thuot East Field airport I noticed a gathering at the community centers and people walking toward the polls with their I.D. cards. Even though much VC activity threatened throughout Vietnam, I have not heard of any incidents that put a damper on the elections. Last night there were a few explosions in Saigon but, generally quiet elsewhere. There was one exception, this province, Lam Dong. Wilbanks told me of six incidents within 24 hours in Lam Dong. He should know he had to fly the missions. (Wilbanks later received the Medal of Honor, Posthumously; on the day I left country).
Returned to camp at 1000 hours in a CV-2 Caribou. The team appeared glad to see me. Was it because I brought mail and vitals or were they in fact glad to see the Dai Uy? I was sure glad to see them. The Caribou is a great little aircraft that goes anywhere and lands anywhere.
September 12, 1966 I'm on guard now. It's 0130 hours. A patrol just called in suspecting VC in Tan Rai village. After they checked it out they found the villagers were still celebrating from the national elections.

I had a long talk with the team. I summarized my leadership principles. It was easy because I had just reviewed Atilla the Hun's principles of war and I put them into my own words. I feel I can apply them in this situation. I especially like the idea of Attila the Hun's nickname the 'scourge of the earth'. I too have picked up a nickname according to my VC intelligence sources, "The Dai Uy who acts and thinks simultaneously". The short form is "Zen Dai Uy". Actually I kind of like it, maybe I can get some mileage out of it in my civil affairs and psychological operations. It was good for me as well to talk to the team members as I have been away for quite some time and we had to bring each other up to date. I have learned and developed my own leadership strategy, which seems to work;

1. Keep the boss informed and pleased, This allows me to do what is best for Tan Rai,
2. Keep a positive attitude,
3. Treat counterparts and subordinates with respect,
4. Listen to subordinates,
5. Think of how to do things better,
6. Be honest with myself and compatriots,
7. Kill VC with a vengeance,
8. Build the economy,
9. Turn the camp over to Vietnamese and
10. Never, never, tell another SF a lie, save those for the legs.

The village chief invited us down for a ceremony at 0900 hours. They killed two buffalo. It took them the normal 45 minutes to kill each one. I coordinated with the priest while they were killing one. He wants a salary for his two catholic nun schoolteachers. I agreed to pay them since they were good with the children, but I would pay them directly. He agreed, not that I would suspect any graft within the Roman Catholic structure, but I did not want to put any unnecessary pressure on his position.

During the ceremony today the woman of the house did something that I had never seen before. She sacrificed three or four pieces of fine Montagnard cloth. She put it on the buffalo's neck after he was killed or I should say while he was dying. I can only postulate that it was to ward off the bad spirits? I took a lot of pictures.

September 14, 1966 Sergeant Vanhorne and I mounted a company-sized operation and met up with my counterpart who also had a company in the AO.

Before departure we gave the customary guidance. "Before operations every weapon has to be broken down, scrubbed with solvent, and oiled. As soon as we get to our night ambush, break 'em down again but make sure your buddy is ready to fire. Make sure everyone's grenade pins are taped down tight; that means. We don't want them catching on branches and going off. Use green tape to secure anything that makes noise. Tape down the swivels."

We were on our way to clear a village from which one of my squads drew fire last night. All night we lobbed mortars in on the VC positions. As we moved south we stopped at the Frenchman's Tea plantation and had a chat. I told him if VC activity continued in his area I would be forced to mortar his tea fields and close him down. He got all choked up about this and started giving me information about the VC. Most of it was worthless but he did confirm former suspicions. Later my interpreter told me the Frenchman paid Taxes to the VC. He had talked with the Frenchman's interpreter. The Frenchman's daughter was easy to single out of the crowd of children playing in the yard. She had blue eyes and brown hair. The Frenchman is married to a Montagnard and is proud of his Euro/Asian off spring. He also asked me, "If I know of a VC who wanted to defect how would one do it?"

I told him, "send the VC to my camp and we would treat him fairly."

We then moved into an ambush position and rested for the night. The Frenchman offered me a nice bed for the night but I refused, not because the VC commander stayed there the night before, as I found out later, but I wanted to be with my troops.

The best way to beat the enemy was to out-guerrilla him. We have to use the jungle to our advantage, use Charlie's sanctuary to beat him at his own game.

September 15,1966 Purple Heart

'SHRAPNEL' We cleared the VC Positions in the village of Ke Tan Bla this morning and made plans to tear down all ammunition storage areas and burn the overhead thatched roofs. I gave the go ahead to clear the buildings of booby traps first. That's when it happened. We took fire from a squad of VC. Sergeant Vanhorne and I fired M-79 rounds into the VC strongholds. There was a double explosion. I was standing up and ZAP. I took a piece of shrapnel in the lower abdomen wall. It knocked me off my feet and I laid about 15 feet from where I got zapped. I was bleeding and stinging from the hot metal inside my stomach. It felt like a baseball hit me. I guess the combination of impact and muscle reaction caused me to be knocked so far. The abdomen is the largest muscle in the body. Vanhorne called for a helicopter to evacuate me to Bao Loc. He did not know how to spell abdomen so he wrote on the med-evac tag, "gunshot six inches above the penis". Once this word got out on the Collins single side-band radio all A-Teams in B-23 heard that Dai Uy Striler got shot in the penis. You can imagine the ribbing I took from my fellow A-Team commanders. Later I ran into friends who thought I was dead. That is an eerie feeling, to say hello, and reply with shock by saying,

"Gosh, I thought you were dead!"

There were times when it seemed that everything within me savored the essence of life just because I had lived so close to death.

Doc Siebert, the navy doctor at Bao Loc, probed around with a nine-inch long wooden probe stick with a cotton swab on the end. It burned as he pushed it into the abdomen wall but then all I felt was pressure, not pain. I could see him push the probe in about three inches as he ordered me to go to the Nha Trang hospital. He reminded me I would be one sick puppy and in a lot of pain. I was in Nha Trang at the 8th General Hospital within the hour. There I had to wait a couple of hours before the surgeon could see me. He put me on Intravenous fluids (IV), injecting potassium chloride and other nutrients. I reckon I was dehydrated. Then they took more x-rays. I then slept for 16 hours and awoke to the normal testing series, blood, temperature, and pulse. The x-ray showed a slug about the size of a .32 caliber round about 2 inches inside the abdomen wall. Doc said it did not penetrate the bladder or intestines and that I was a lucky man. I was starving and I finally talked the doctor into letting me eat real food.

Also I saw a Viet Cong in the bed across from me. He must have had heart problems along with all of the other wounds. The doctors and nurses were cutting his chest open, massaging his heart and beating him purposefully. It seemed to be a futile effort but that did not stop the intensity. I don't think the VC lived through it. I ate my rice, beans, jello and bread and slept more. The VC was gone when I awoke. Another patient who was missing a leg replaced him and the foot was gone from the other leg. He was either comatose or in a deep stupor.

September 16, 1966 The Doctor decided to leave the shrapnel in me and not operate. I am recovering rapidly. I'm a little sore around the wound. I moved to the recovery ward from the emergency ward. Saw Master Sergeant Jim Shoulders, my A-team sergeant from Germany, tonight. Jim is undoubtedly a great soldier. His charismatic leadership style is surpassed by few. Looks like he will be evacuated to Tokyo, then probably to the States.

Captain John J. Truffa Jr. and Henderson and the Chaplain came by to visit me today. I saw Gene Tafoya, my demolition's sergeant. It looks like he had malaria after all. He appeared weak, pale and lost over 40 pounds. He is going to Cam Rhan Bay for three weeks recovery. That means I'll be short Americans again. Where is this idea that an A-team consist of 12 Americans, that's hogwash. Operationally, I seem to have only five at any one time; due to injuries, malaria, and emergency leaves. Also saw pilots from the 92nd aviation. They agreed to fly me to my camp if I could get discharged from the hospital. I asked the nurse if I could be discharged. She could not authorize it. I have to figure a way to get out of this hospital. My team needs me.

September 17, 1966 At 0700 hours this AM I told the nurse I was leaving.

She said,

"If you leave I will count you as AWOL."

"What will you do with me Ma'am, send me to Vietnam?"

She glared at me,

"You Special Forces studs are all alike you think you're so macho."

After hearing that I knew I made the right decision in getting out of there.

Captain Beardsly picked me up at 0730 hours and we headed for the airfield. Finally flew out at 1500 hours to Nhon Co (A 235). Looked over their camp and got an L-19 back to Tan Rai. I am going to invest in the latest soldiers deposit plan at 10% interest and encourage my men to do the same. That is incredible.

September 18, 1966 I flew my operational area with Captain Wesby. According to intelligence reports, there was a suspected Company of VC northwest of camp. Their reported strength was 41. We did not see traces of them from the air. I will mount an operation in the morning and see if we can flush them out.

At 1400 hours the Tan Rai village chief invited us down to celebrate the arrival of my three new Americans and my return from the hospital. That went on until about 1800 hours. We all got tipsy on Nam Pai. I had all the kids singing, "When the Saint's go Marching In". We all barfed at least once. The villagers love to see the Americans puke. After a few drinks we lost our dignity, we then puked through the bamboo slats in the floor of the Long house rather than walk outside. Seeing us in such a human way tends to bring us off our pedestals. Otherwise they hold us in such high esteem its hard to communicate. I guess they feel we are like them if we puke. I went out one time to throw up and on the way back my team sergeant Jim Nabors met me at the door throwing up all over the floor. Paradoxically there was TOP our hero, the one who walks on water, our leader exposing that he is actually a human capable of doing something human. He got a standing ovation from the curious 'Yards.' Being somewhat new he did not realize he was endearing himself to the yards for life now that he appeared to be vulnerable and human. Can you imagine the stench the following day? They poured us in bed and Sergeant Vanhorne volunteered to get the company ready to go on operations for me early in the morning. Therefore I could sleep until departure.

September 19, 1966 At 0200 hours I was awakened by Vanhorne, who quickly reminded me it would soon be time to depart on operation to locate and engage VC. My head was throbbing and I did not stop up-chucking and then dry heaving until we finally moved into an ambush site four hours later. We rested for about an hour. Then a 5-man squad of VC hit us. Two of my Strikers were injured, one shot in the foot and the other in the leg. I gave my first morphine shot at that time and looking the young Striker in the eye told him he would be alright. If nothing else, it helped him psychologically. We pursued the VC but they broke contact and only left a trail of blood where my machine gunner must have hit one of them. I then brought in a helicopter to evacuate my two casualties. This all took place within 40 minutes. As the adrenaline subsided my hang over became evident again. I was sick. After eating I felt better. My new man reacted well under fire for the first time. He is the team medic. Chuck Orona is a leader's dream come true. He has a positive attitude. He is physically and emotionally strong. He is in shape, mission oriented and smart. Above all he can think on his feet and the Yards love him because he is empathetic and a medicine man. I'm six foot two and he towers over me. He reminds me of a professional basketball player.

Our M-60 machine gun is the most effective weapon in the platoon. Its rate of fire and killing power is coveted by all line troops. Therefore they don't mind carrying the extra weight. There is one Yard in particular, bigger than most always seems to be the one carrying it. In the event of enemy contact, it is critical that we are able to deploy the M-60 to the point of contact. If this proves possible we often gain fire superiority and overrun the enemy's position.

While my day was full of activity, Pope Paul VI appealed to world leaders today in the encyclical, Christi Matri, to end the war in Vietnam. I wish he could will it that easily. I had the opportunity to see him while I was in Rome a few short years ago. I remember my strict catholic upbringing at Sacred Heart Parochial School in Festus, Missouri, where the nuns tried to convince us that it would happen if we prayed for it.

The red ribbons and scarves came out today and were tied on the barrels of the carbines. I suppose it is not only for protection of the Buddha but also to commemorate the FULRO uprising of two years ago. This is the anniversary date. The Montagnard rebellion took place from 19 to 28 September 1964.

September 20, 1966 I listened all night for an air strike, which was to occur before we attacked our main objective, which is a village with suspected VC in it. We saw a lot of Tiger tracks on the trail as we moved toward the objective, also a dead cow buffalo with her calf still sucking at a dead udder. Buzzards were lurking overhead waiting for us to leave. I reckon the VC killed I and planned to come back for a feast. We must have spoiled their plan. At 1030 hours the point man ran into a fork in the trail and a fresh trail. I told the company commander to secure the area and run patrols out to find out which way the VC went. Suddenly we saw the VC squad and every gun around opened fire. Finally after everything settled down, I saw one dead VC laying about 10 feet from me. Apparently there were two of them. One got away. I sent a platoon after the other one. I fired about twenty M-79 grenade launcher rounds in that direction to give the Yards confidence pursuing the enemy. I would fire then throw my hand back and my grenadier would slap another grenade in my hand. That explosion certainly encourages the Strikers to charge at the VC; otherwise they are hesitant to advance in the face of enemy fire.

I believe the Strikers would lay flat on the ground and let the VC get away, if it wasn't for the M-79 explosions. We searched the VC and found he was a North Vietnamese soldier. He was carrying three 60 mm mortar rounds and a PPSH 41 assault rifle. His uniform was ratty and he possessed little, no money or personal belongings. No friendly casualties this time. That's what happens when we see them first.

Swept through the objective and saw nothing. Walked back across the swamp and set up an ambush for the night. Experienced many leeches today. Those pestilent little parasites drop from trees going for the body heat. They come up from moist areas and in certain locals are literally and figuratively everywhere. My personal defense is to wear no underwear or socks because they hold in the heat and take longer to dry. We have periodic leech checks and put cigarettes to these ubiquitous pests. That usually breaks their tenacious hold although there is a risk there because they may barf into the pore before dropping off.

September 21, 1966 When the column stopped I walked a diagonal to get to the head of the formation where Chuck was. I inadvertently walked across a yellow-jacket nest and was attacked by hundreds of these flying sting machines. I had to pull my jungle fatigues off to get them off my body. I was stung no less than 27 times. I thought I was a goner. I told Chuck to be prepared to med-evac me and keep an eye on me. I slept for about half an hour and woke up feeling alright. They must not have been poisonous.

Ran across an old VC camp. We had dinner there then moved on. Saw traces of VC all over. I would like to think they are moving out of my area. If they have not yet, they should because we're getting bigger and more formidable. We are gaining more and more control giving the Yards more confidence.

September 22, 1966 I had breakfast in bed this morning at 0400 hours. Sergeant Orona fixed me a cup of coffee before we moved out for camp. I wondered why he was so nice to me? At any rate the coffee was OK. My hammock swayed gently as I drank my coffee in harmony not spilling a drop.

We arrived back at the camp at 1030 hours. The hot shower felt good. The food was excellent, but my stomach shrunk so I could not consume all that I intended. That seems to happen after a 3 to 5 day operation. We instructed our cooks Cookie and Pecker-head, two young Indigenous tribesmen how to make potato salad. However we forgot to tell them the difference between sweet potatoes and Idaho reds. You guessed it, as we looked at the meal the potato salad was made out of sweet potatoes. We just ate it and told the cooks how good it was. Coming off operations, anything is good.

We must be winning the war with all of the commitments that we are getting from higher headquarters. It took me 20 minutes to read all of the incoming messages that had stacked up over the four-day period.

23 September 1966 I've been asked if I want defoliation in my Area of Operation.

I said, "no."

The concept is; US planes defoliate dense jungle areas to deny cover and concealment to the enemy. It just seems too high tech for me. I'd rather do it my way.

I have been busy ever since I came back to camp. Sure has been a long 48-hour period. I received my psychology and philosophy books yesterday in the mail. Hot diggidy! I have a lot of reading ahead of me to prepare myself for my Masters degree. I fixed potato pancakes for the men tonight. Heidi sent a box of dried potatoes. They loved them but they were not as good as when she fixes them.

I have been reading more of Confucius. Here are some of my favorites:

" Great man seeks to be slow of speech but quick of action. "

" The parents' age must always be known both as a source of joy and a source of dread."

" Great man's attitude toward the world is such that he shows no preferences, but he is prejudiced in favor of justice. "

" Shall I tell you what knowledge is? It is to know both what one knows and what one does not know. "

The Yards whether educated or not, believe exactly what their ancestral leaders pass on to them in the form of stories. They seem to believe in the morality professed by Confucius. Above all, they bow to the spirits – to the spirits of their ancestors and to many others; to the spirits of great men of the past; to spirits of the sky and of the fields, of trees and of animals; to spirits good and evil. In the most important matters of their village decisions they consult sub-chiefs, mediums, sorcerers, medicine-men and astrologers-to learn what to do, when to do it, and when not to. The biggest emphasis is on when not to. Now I am beginning to understand why on some days I can get things done easily with the Yards and other days, no way.

Beware of the inauspicious, bad spirit days they tell me. They appear about three to four days a month at which time you have to accept the idea that nothing gets accomplished. When I had AWOLs that must have been during inauspicious days. It appears the day's activities are tied to astrology and the lunar cycle. We Westerners can't ignore their beliefs for we are relentlessly seeking truth just as they are. However we approach it from, what we call a logical, scientific model, rather than this Ying Yang approach.

September 24, 1966 Two F100 fighter pilots came into camp today. We scrambled to get in the correct uniform thinking a General was with them. Captain Voge and Captain Fogle visited and stayed all night. The cleanliness and healthy living habits we practice impressed Fogle. I'm not sure what he expected? He said he could sleep and eat more restful here than in Saigon. I trained two Yards to fire the 4.2 mortar and directed them to fire during the night. The visitors thought it a bit noisy.

Fogle said,

"Ray I bet you will miss this place!"

He was referring to the professional but friendly atmosphere and the way every one gets along. I surprised myself with my provocatively reflective moment.

"I've made a lot of friends here. It is they whom I will miss."

That satisfied him but I was then thinking of everything that had happened, the growth of the camp, the leadership, the crisis', the joys and sorrows. Deep in my thoughts was all the emotion of the hard work to get to this point and the hard working dedicated SF team along with the Yard leadership that did it. It was as if I was talking to my inner self and being outwardly reflective and inwardly emotive at the same time.

Recruits came in today, seventy-four all together. I had sent out an American and LLDB and an impressive Yard to the village and they recruited for several days and returned with this selected group. Good job guys. I wonder how many are VC sympathizers? Now for the weeding out process and training. Lots to do. I gave them my standard welcome speech.

September 25, 1966 The pilots left. An operation went out and we recruited sixty-one more Strikers. I am reading "ASIA NOW" by Edwin Reischauer. Who by the way, seems to be the only American author on Asia besides Bernard Shaw that we can get our hands on. My how limited we are at this juncture in history. His book is an excellent insightful comprehensive rundown on Asia today. A bit colored red, but interesting. I have the strength of 601 Strikers now plus numerous civilian workers. That is a good-sized battalion.

I flew over a part of my operational area today. There was a report by the national police of 400 VC. Consequently, I sent a company out to check it out. We saw nothing.

September 26, 1966 A C-123 came in today and complained about the soft runway. Of course it is. We received 5 inches of rain last night. The lumbering aircraft with the pop belly settled a foot into the mud. Major Gillette came in and looked around. I'm always glad to see him. I enjoy showing him the progress Tan Rai has made. I undoubtedly have the finest Americans in the Army. I wish I could do more for them, to enhance their careers.

September 27, 1966 A CV-2 brought a movie projector in late this evening. Our fighter friends put on a show for us, they buzzed camp and pumped 20-mm rounds on the old remains of the Frenchman's house, our registration point, 200 meters away. That's where Mr. Charles hangs out on occasion. We had reports he may be there. They hit it with surprising precision. Then they peeled off and rolled a few times. My Strikers observed in awe. I'll send a patrol out to check damages in the morning.

September 28, 1966 A CV-2 came in today bringing Colonel Mueller and the mail. Can't get the sound to work on the movie projector. Seventy-one more recruits signed up today. I sat down with Team Sergeant Nabors and K'Gee, the Battalion Commander, went over tactics and established more refined policy today. As we expand and build, our simple policies need re-evaluation for efficacy. Everything is going smoothly. We are expecting VIP's tomorrow. Jim Nabors is undoubtedly the greatest team sergeant in Special Forces. He brings with him Korean War experience. Calm, cool, intelligent, honest, good values, extremely fair and professional. One could not ask for a better team Sergeant. The men look up to him more than I have seen in quite awhile. He brings stability, team effort and confidence to the force.

September 29, 1966 The National Police arrested two of my Strikers in Bao Loc today. They were on the known VC list. My intelligence Sergeant knew this and was observing them and getting valuable information from them. He tracked where they went, whom they talked with, and their every move. Now I have to re-strategize, locate and observe other VC in my force and employ them the same way. The word will get out that they are in jail so Charley will be looking for replacements. I hope I can identify replacements for my own net. My executive officer, Lieutenant Chet Jones, came back today from a supply requisition trip to DaLat and Nha Trang. He was quite successful. What a can do attitude he has! He never fails.

A full Colonel RF/ PF (Regional and Provincial Forces) senior advisor came in today. I gave him the $3.00 tour. Colonel Charles M. Simpson III, DCO (Deputy Commanding Officer), Colonel Eleazar Parmly, IV, (Commander C2), Major Gillette (Commander B-23) and his counterpart, Dai Uy Thong came in also. I gave them the $6.00 tour. Simpson said he's visited 90 camps and at this camp he was impressed with the cleanliness, organization and morale. He saw three things with which he was impressed; first, the company commanders and Battalion commanders working in the Staff tent and the other two he said I knew. I believe he was referring to the homing beacon, and the briefing about turning the Regional and Popular forces over to the South Vietnamese and possibly our construction projects.
September 30, 1966 This is payday for the Strikers. The Americans get paid tomorrow. I had heard of one VC suspect in Mnrong Sekang, so I sent a platoon to pick him up. He squealed on seven others, mostly women. We picked them up. It turned out to be 5 women and 22 children. I fed them and secured them in the village and will question them tomorrow. CIDG (Civilian Irregular Defense Group) chow came in today. This is a much-awaited event, I will explain later.
We received a coded message that Colonel Francis "Blackjack" Kelly, needing volunteers to form and command a Mobile Guerrilla Force (M.G.F.). Operationally lead by Americans. This is the strategy we have been using. I hope it works at his level.

October 1, 1966 Thung Uy Minh brought his wife and family in on the helicopter. The operation was slow and disorganized in getting out of here. The helicopter didn't show. I hope this slow start isn't indicative of how the operation will go. I guess everything has been going too smoothly to expect it to continue. The stigma for this operation as I see it could well be the LLDB first sergeant. He's a little wishy-washy and disorganized, unfortunately he's in a key decision making slot. I'll have to see what I can do about ousting him. He has too much control of the store funds. I don't trust him. I believe he over-charges the Yards.

It is dark and overcast. I suspect the rain will come pouring down soon. I was going to DaLat yesterday but now I'm down to five Americans so I'll wait until I get more. There is an A-Team leader meeting coming up on the 8th in Buon Ma Thuot, maybe I'll go then. I won $25 playing poker tonight with team members.

October 2, 1966 Our new jeep came in today on a CV-2, also ammunition. I'd say we are a strong well-defended, well-supplied camp. It's amazing the changes that have been made since June. I can hardly believe them myself. Did I tell you? I showed my cooks how to make potato pancakes. They really try hard to please us, and intrinsically all they expect is an occasional word of praise—and of course, pay. They work for nominal wages, about $35 a month. We've trained them to do everything. Since they provide us basic needs, we can concentrate on leading the force. One of the 'Yards' knows how to run the movie projector. They light the fires and clean up. We have two pets at the present time in camp. One is "Oink", the pig, obviously, but since he hasn't seen another pig since he was two weeks old, he thinks he's a dog and an American. He only makes friends with Americans, not Vietnamese or Montagnards. He walks all around one tent but knows never to come inside.

We keep him around because when he hears incoming mortars he squeals and dashes for cover. He learned this at an outpost in Di Linh. We purchased him in June and now he is one of us. He already saved lives. Our other pet is a falcon, named Scarecrow. He's domesticated and eats out of our hands. We keep him around because we can't get rid of him.

October 3, 1966 The operation made contact with a large squad, approximately eight VC, had a small firefight and when the smoke cleared, killed one VC, captured one, plus two carbines and rucksacks. Unfortunately we had three friendly casualties: one in the buttocks, one in the thigh and one in the head. I told them to bring the captured VC to my location for questioning, but by the time he arrived on the helicopter he was near death from shock, so I had Bac Xi stabilize him and sent him on to Buon Ma Thuot. The helicopter missed the trees on takeoff by inches. The pilot called back and said that was the closest call he had ever had.

Two C-123's came in today. The runway was muddy. It rained yesterday and all last night. They asked about the softness of the runway and we told them about the record of C-123's coming in — three landed, two got stuck. They laughed but came in anyway on the second pass.

October 4, 1966 One injured Striker died.

Sergeant First Class Barnes' bunker caught on fire last night. I called an alert and had all bunkers checked for sabotage — nothing.

The operation spotted over 150 VC. When Wesby heard that he dashed out and flew quickly in his L-19. He is out over the area calling in an air strike as I write this entry. The operation is being re-supplied today with two days of rice. They should be back in camp tomorrow. I plan to get the dead Striker back today. We'll have to inform his family and pay gratuity pay and have a funeral. The B team wanted to send the dead VC back to me. I told them, "Don't bother."

SECTION FOUR: LOGISTICS

CHAPTER 9 LOGISTICS

October 5, 1966 The operation came in today. The general did not show up; too much rain. Pay officer came in to pay the Americans their monthly salary. A few interesting occurrences happened to the operational unit. Remember the incident in World War II when the Americans marched past the Germans and didn't realize it was the enemy until it was too late and they had already disappeared out of site? Well, the operation flanked one side of a road and the VC, many of them, flanked the other side and they walked past each other in a daze. Also the one VC killed was eleven years old, the other fifteen. The young one is believed to have wounded two and killed one of my Strikers. On the way into the operational area the point man saw a truck with six VC in it. The VC opened fire and resultantly my Strikers fired, killing one and capturing two. I turned the captives over to Sector for questioning. I gave my second intravenous injection (IV) to the one VC who was wounded in the shoulder. His veins were fragile and even though I inserted the needle in the vein, it would collapse and I would have to do it again. He had about five holes in him from my attempts and the collapsed veins, when I finally got the IV started and we put him on the airplane. My doctor finally arrived and dressed the wound. He had a good pulse so he'll be all right. Bac Xi told everyone I saved the VC's life.

I believe he was only saying that to make me feel good about giving the IV. Another incidental thing happened, a few of the Strikers recognized the VC. They had lived next door in Di Linh.

I see where Colonel Parmly got the Distinguished Service Cross for Bravery (DSC) for his action at Duc Co.

I just read the article about Major Fisher and his extreme heroism in Readers Digest, August 1966 - " A Pilot is Down." I used to read those articles and never believed they were possible, but now that I know the characters involved, I know it is true. I also know it's possible.

October 6, 1966 A Company sized force left on operation last night at 0100 hours. No contact yet. Raining again, I closed the airstrip to C-123's. It is too soft and I have to repair it when it gets ruts in it. The damage done was large ruts and holes. It will need to be bulldozed when it dries up.

With this increase in Strikers I am sure we have a pretty good number of VC infiltrators or sympathizers in camp now and I intend to weed them out. I need a stronger counter intelligence net. Although the net is risky to operate, it may be the fastest way to break down the VC infrastructure. We identify the VC and pay them to be our agents as well. I visited all the companies earlier tonight. It is my periodic good-will tour.

It is 2100 hours and my element on operations just made contact with a carrying party, probably two or three VC carrying supplies, ammunition and medical supplies. They won't be able to determine exact results until morning. It is pitch black outside.

October 7, 1966 Flew to Buon Ma Thuot today for the monthly meeting of A detachment commanders. Sat around and talked to all the team leaders and team sergeants. Saw Mr. Johnson, my Chinese food contractor. He seems to be a real entrepreneur. He had Heidi's painting finished. I gave him a small black and white photo of her earlier. I told him her hair and eye color. He painted it on plywood. Looks great. More like a German with a bit of Vietnamese in her features. It's 18" by 24" in size.

October 8, 1966 I mailed the picture along with oriental gifts home today.

Just prior to the meeting I got word that the operation made contact with a company sized element. Needless to say I was concerned.

"What's going on?" I asked.

"First Platoon spotted a couple of Charlie's approaching their sector."

"What were they wearing?" I asked.

"Black PJs and AKs."

"They wearing rucks?" I asked, trying to determine the situation.

"Yes."

"That means they are on the move and don't know we are in the area. The local VC probably would not have rucks."

In this area the local VC were organized into six-to-twelve-man cells. They were usually responsible for maintaining the base camps serving as guides for Viet Cong and North Vietnamese Army (N.V.A.) mainforce units infiltrating through the area, and providing security when their camps were occupied.

If the VC were from a base camp that was occupied by a VC or N.V.A. battalion or regimental sized unit, their next move would probably be to deploy against us. If large units were present in the area there was a good chance that they would come from regiments of the 9th Viet-Cong Division - - the same regiments we had tangled with a few weeks earlier. If they were N.V.A. main-force units they could be Balo Company or L66 or one of the A companies. We also knew that the enemy could mobilize and field a number of platoons or company sized units against us. These were under the command of the Viet-Cong Province Committee and were usually difficult to deal with because of their extensive knowledge of the local terrain. I would much rather deal with the foreigners because my men knew this terrain like the back of their hand.

At first they asked for a reaction force, then extraction, finally we got air cover over them and an air strike. They must have felt outnumbered to request all that power. That is unusual especially for Jones. He is a seasoned warrior. They reported the situation as being less serious after air support arrived. I sure was relieved. Charley surrounded them and if it hadn't been for the air strike, well, I don't know? I doubt that I could have gotten a reaction force out to them in time. Reaction force operations are risky and treacherous anyhow because of the possibility of being ambushed along the way. When you move rapidly and the enemy knows where you are coming from your risk goes up. So I guess the air strike saved them.

The meeting was a typical monthly meeting, everyone reported on their camp and the B team commander and staff bestowed upon us their observations. Seems like VC forces are strengthening.

October 9, 1966 Flew out of Buon Ma Thuot to Nha Trang at 0800 hours, made one stop in DaLat. Rode with Don Sweigart who commands an A-team on the coastal area. I introduced him to Charley Diep, my Nha Trang contractor. We went out and had a great time. Don has been in some tight scrapes. He showed me a few scars creasing his rib cage and his foot. Says he's exhausted. I think he should go on leave and get away awhile. He's been on one operation after another, just like me when I first took over the A-Team.

October 10, 1966 Saw Gene Tosh and Sergeant First Class Quimby who I'm trying to get assigned to my team as intelligence sergeant. Quimby was on my underwater recovery team in Europe. He is a professional scuba diver with nerves of steel. He recovered a few bombs on one mission we went on in Germany by request of the German government. Gene Tosh was telling us how he broke his leg in a combat action while jumping off a bridge.

Requisitioning supplies took up the biggest part of the day for what is needed at camp. Also checked on my team member's awards, little progress.

October 11, 1966 I got a CV-2 aircraft diverted from Nhon Co to Tan Rai today. I commandeered a freezer plus fresh meat. It's amazing how much you can get for captured weapons. Those REMFs (rear support troops) will pay any price. I had to fly into An Loc then Nhon Co, where I picked up cement then flew to Tan Rai. Saw Sergeant Tafoya and Sergeant Griffin while in route.

October 12, 1966 Got the work details organized today, completed the team house floor, brought in a C-123 that had a three-quarter ton truck on it that I requisitioned a few days ago. We were expecting three CV-2's, but only one showed. Played poker, still no noise on the projector.

October 13,1966 Received CIDG food today. Typically once a week two CV-2s brings greens, Nouc Mam (fish sauce), and five cows for the five companies to be split equally. The food is for the soldiers and dependents. I probably feed some VC also. Got to keep the VC healthy, if I want a worthy opponent. Right? Moved into my new underground room. It's 6 x 6 feet and located right in the middle of my operations bunker in the inner perimeter. I have a canvas-folding cot for a bed, a folding chair, and a dresser. On the earth wall hangs a radio, M-16, flak vest, and rucksack. It's cool, and damp as the walls are mostly laterite type mud, or as they say in Missouri, red clay. My bed is covered with a camouflage poncho liner and a mosquito net draped over that. It's livable; especially knowing there is 24 inches of protection overhead. Just so someone doesn't throw a hand grenade into the air vent. I'll be up tight.

The Secretary of Defense, Robert S. McNamara, after making his eighth fact-finding mission to South Vietnam said, "Military operations have progressed very satisfactorily since 1965," but conceded that, "Progress is very slow indeed in the pacification program." He should have visited Tan Rai. Pacification is a constant theme along with keeping the VC under wrap.

October 14, 1966 A Company sized operation departed at 0500 hours this morning. Colonel Bill Simpson came in on an Otter aircraft. I showed him around and gave him a briefing. This is his second visit. He asks tough and pertinent questions and always seems to be impressed at our progress. A CV-2 also shuttled in. I invited the Province chief and senior American advisor to come visit on Sunday to get acquainted. My counterpart and I had our differences last night, lack of coordination, plus his first sergeant lied to him and was afraid to stand behind his word. I wanted to send the reconnaissance platoon with 'A' company. He didn't want to for some reason. I insisted and they moved out smartly this morning.

Two AWOL's that returned to camp turned out to be VC. I suspect I have a lot more Viet Cong in camp. My counterpart, Trung Uy Minh, and I were talking about VC in camp and we both agree they are here, but we don't agree on the number. I think it could be as high as 10 %, he says 2%.

Trung Uy says, "on many local ambushes the Strikers let the VC walk right by without making contact; some of the VC are brothers and cousins of the Strikers."

I guess it's an unwritten code to avoid contact if possible, unless an American is along to insist that they do battle. Some families are torn between north and south beliefs and the men get jobs wherever they can. They have to support their family. Sometimes they are forced to join the VC. I think I'll identify the VC then put them as point men on a night patrol and see how much action they stir up. The point man has about a 50% chance of getting zapped if he makes contact. If it's an ambush his chances of getting zapped go up precipitously, like ninety percent.

October 15, 1966 It's Saturday and I gave the troops off a half day. They deserve it after three months of working 16 hours a day, seven days a week. I flew around my operational area this morning making a reconnaissance for the operation on Monday. I'll take 'B' company out for a search-and-destroy mission and join up with Sergeant Roger Temple who has a company out now. Should get a few VC and I'm looking for a supply cache. An informant indicated there was one in that area.

Bao Loc had a walk-in VC. Now that is the way to prevent loss of life, to have them walk in and give themselves up. I don't know what the details are yet. At any rate he confirmed T 6's headquarters location. That's west of us. Supposed to be a headquarters for several provinces. I'm anxious to get more details. They might put American troops in there. Bao Loc flew over the area and the informant pointed out VC hospital locations, enemy troop areas, and training areas. Might be a breakthrough for us.

October 16, 1966 Lieutenant Colonel Gillette, recently promoted, dropped by today after he heard we made contact. My company reported that a reinforced platoon was sitting on the hill watching them. My company could not engage in a firefight because Charley was just out of range. Captain Wesby flew over them and called in an air strike. He came by camp and picked me up. I helped him call in the jets. I didn't see any dead VC's as we flew in for the final assessment. Sergeant Temple, who was on the ground near the air strike, reported blood on the trails when he swept through.

Tomorrow at 0400 hours I take another company out for five days. We are looking for a VC platoon in Ke Tan Bla. They were reported there today. Also a rice cache for VC is supposed to be near Ke Tan Bla.

October 17, 1966 Moved out at 0400 hours. It was pitch black. It's the first time this company moved out at night and is still learning advanced tactics. It was disorganized to say the least. After a few miles it became evident we were using precious energy and getting nowhere. I told them to wait until daylight then we would move again. We went about seven miles cross-country and suddenly we found this beautiful rice meadow. I peered through the binoculars to find at first one Montagnard, a lady, bathing in a small pond contingent to a lovely green rice field. Then there were seven all together all around the hutches and around the fields. We approached and found that the VC came into the area regularly to get rice, twenty kilograms every day. Charley would occasionally deflower the ladies. It doesn't take much figuring to know that's enough rice for two VC platoons. So we set up ambushes and waited. Meanwhile A Company was operating north of us as I mentioned yesterday.   At about 1400 hours the hillside opened up with automatic fire. I was in the village at the time. I ran one hundred meters towards the action and found three dead VC who had gotten between our two companies.

The VC were laying in one heap, as they must have been very close together when my companies opened up on them. Their weapons were fairly well maintained and had been shot recently indicating some discipline and leadership. The Strikers said they wounded many more VC but couldn't find any blood trails so we joined up and spent the night on the hilltop, with ambushes set on three sides.

October 18, 1966 After a normal rice and dried fish breakfast and just before we were to move out a congregation from the village of B' Dru wanted to talk to the Dai Uy. They came up to me rather cautiously with all kinds of bows and handshakes and kissing my hands and boots and asked if we could resettle them to Bao Loc. They said the VC were taking all their rice, taking liberties with their women and insulting village elders. That began our quest for the next 48 hours. I called Sector and couldn't get support. They said it would be two weeks before they could accept that many Yards. I sensed there was not much urgency when it comes to the Yards. That made me mad. So we started moving them anyway.

I radioed Sector,

"I am coming in with the whole village and you better get your act together."

Surprisingly just after that radio transmission, my radio went on the blink. I guess it knew what the reply from Sector was going to be. I told the villagers to take only bare essentials. The word did not get translated the way I intended it for later I saw tables, chairs, pigs, Nam Pai and water jugs, crossbows, chickens and rice being carried along with the children. I guess in their perception these items were their bare essentials. By 1500 hours we moved 2 miles to another Frenchmen's coffee plantation.

He invited the Americans to feast with him. Because darkness was soon setting in we decided to move to Bao Loc in the morning. It is a long haul, especially with all that equipment and the old people, convalescents, and children. It's about nine miles on foot through VC territory. Before going to bed I broke out my acetate-covered map and spread it on the ground to determine the best route with that large group.

"What's our route of march?" Dai Uy inquired Roger.

"We'll decide in the morning."

I went to bed early.

October 19, 1966 After long hours of deliberation the village council finally decided to send only seventy-seven of the strong Montagnards and leave behind the old women and children. A total of 275 villagers stayed behind. That made our movement easier. I could just see us carrying babies, old people, plus our weapons and rucks, which were full with four days supply of food and ammunition. Plus I was not sure if the Province Chief would care for them on such short notice.

We had no contact with the VC, fortunately, with the exception of a few sniper rounds, which didn't hit anyone. We closed in on Bao Loc at 1300 hours. I talked with the Province Chief. He was not pleased but did take the people off our hands. We then conducted a forced march on to Tan Rai, which was another seven miles. Everyone's feet were smoking and I know we had as many blisters as we had feet, over 600. It's good to be back in camp.

Colonel 'Blackjack' Kelly, commander of the 5th Special Forces, and Colonel Parmly, the C detachment commander are expected in tomorrow.

I received my Purple Heart with certificate when I got back to camp, signed by the Secretary of the Army, Stanley Resor, himself. The action was from a previous operation in September.

October 21, 1966 Flew to Buon Ma Thuot today to coordinate operations. Upon my return I had two new men assigned to the team. Sergeant First Class Harold W. Coon who is an intelligence sergeant, and Specialist 4th Class Eugene A. Tafoya, Demolitionist, who actually is not new but returning after convalescing from malaria. I was extremely excited to get them both. Coon because he is a little older, wiser, and a total volunteer. He had a good civilian job but gave it up to volunteer to come over here. Tafoya is good to have back because he is a real crafty fighter and knows the force. Also had a letter from President Johnson. The first Presidential inquiry I have had. I heard of other teams receiving Congressionals but not Presidentials. I nervously tour it open to find out Tafoya's mother wrote president Johnson and said Gene had not written for a long time, over a year. I sat down with him and he finally wrote a page. I could not understand the Spanish but I personally mailed it and answered the presidential inquiry to that effect. Did not hear anything after that so I guess the inquiry was answered satisfactorily.

Sent an operation out to secure the village of B' Dru to keep the VC from getting the rice that the villagers left behind. Also have put out a company Northwest of camp to prevent infiltration.   At 1200 hours today a battalion plus two companies of VC were sighted straight west of the camp five miles. They were carrying 75-mm recoilless and 81-mm mortars. As a result, I put all Americans underground while sleeping. I increased the security and rehearsed everyone on alert procedures to include the dependents in the village. Also fired a few Harassing and Interdicting (H and I) rounds from both 4.2 mortars. Charley is planning something. I can feel it in my bones. I don't know what yet. Maybe he's still mad because we have been killing his people and cutting off his rice supply and social opportunities.

I paid Mr. Johnson, my contractor, 100,000 piasters toward the CIDG bill today, also picked up 2,000,000 Piasters for the pay roll. Talked to Colonel Parmly for awhile at lunch about the VC around this area.

October 22, 1966 Was a long quiet night. Our forces, NQ 23, moved into the village at 1500 hours today and are taking up defensive positions. Charley hasn't been there yet. Six villagers were getting the remainder of their things out. My other company survived the night without getting attacked.

We validated another VC in the strike force. My intelligence sergeant was already trailing him.

"How did you detect him?" I asked SFC Harold W. Coon.

"It was easy," he said, "the VC was suffering from malnutrition and when we put the metal detector on him he lit up like a Christmas tree."

"He had been handling weapons and denied it. His 'friends' were not really his friends. From all that we deducted he was VC."

I commented, "He might be a replacement for the two in jail. The B team wants him but I want to keep him under observation a while to break his net."

"Roger that Sir."

October 23, 1966 One Company returned today. One is leaving tomorrow morning. I'm sending Lieutenant Jones and my new intelligence sergeant, Sergeant First Class Coon. Jones should train him well. I don't think Coon needs much training, he seems more mature and experienced. We'll check him out under fire. It should be a good operation. We finally got our projector back and we're watching movies again with sound, beats poker for the time being. After living without the movies for so long, I get a guilty feeling when I watch them because I know I could be reading or writing instead.

I'll never get my psychology and philosophy books read now. Received a letter from Heidi today. Sounds like she's well organized and ready to come to the states from Germany. I'm anxious for her. I know she'll like it. That will be her first time in the USA.

The new pilot who holds the rank of major brought the mail and a film in today. I'm trying to get a helicopter for tomorrow to take supplies into the village. Fired the 4.2 mortar at a few VC that sniped on the returning company. We lobbed about six rounds in on the suspected location. Maybe we got them, maybe we didn't. They stopped sniping and that's what mattered at the time. We taped the fire commands for training purposes to replay and learn lessons. I plan to cut a tape of camp activities for historical purposes.

October 24, 1966 Three of my Americans stayed outside of camp past dark last night. I was pissed. We had a long talk. I let them know how disappointed I was in their behavior. I don't think it will happen again. It also gave me an opportunity to let them know where they stand. Today both operations made contact with VC, one with a platoon and one with a squad. We put mortars in on the VC. Charley abducted three of the women and forced them to have sex and when he was finished turned them loose and fired on my operation. Testy isn't he? Levity or humility? That is Charley's inimitable Psychological Operations plan, I guess. Sergeant Coon asked the three ladies, what they thought about being raped by the VC.

They said, "It wasn't bad," giggled and covered up their betel nut stained and filed down teeth.

I'm supposed to get two 105-mm howitzers in my camp. I hope I get them soon. It would increase the range of our operations by several thousand meters. It would be a real kick to learn about the artillery commands and operations first hand using my own 105-mm howitzers. We wouldn't have to count on air support.

We sure could give Charley problems!

October 25, 1966 One Company returned. The other got surrounded by three companies of VC. We called in an air strike about 50 meters from their position and the VC broke contact. I expect Charley will come back during the night, especially if he realizes he has us outnumbered three to one. We'll be standing by on the radio just in case. We had two Strikers wounded: one in the leg and the other in the back and neck. They reported three dead VC and three captured weapons. The medical evacuation helicopter couldn't make it in. It was too dark and the drop zone was not secured. So the chopper flew back to camp and the crew is spending the night here. They'll execute the extraction first thing in the morning. I gave the aviators and crew black pajamas and their eyes lit up with delight. I also sent out a reaction company. The two elements should link up some time tomorrow morning. The moon is out and they should be able to move swiftly.

October 26, 1966 1966 Heidi's 25th Birthday

The wounded Striker died in the night. The two companies linked up early in the morning. Had contact off and on all day - small elements. Charley doesn't want us in that area for some reason. I just got an intelligence report that he has an anti-aircraft gun three miles north of the area at which my company is located. Wes isn't going to like that. The more Charley tries to keep us out, the more we want to go in to see what he is hiding. Got the med-evac chopper in finally and the gunships stayed around most of the day just in case. They discovered a battalion VC training area: tunnels, firing ranges, punji stakes, fighting positions and mess halls. Also found a combat hamlet.

I heard President Johnson flew to Cam Rhan Bay for a surprise visit.

October 27, 1966 We purchased a wooden casket for the Striker. The candles burned, drums twanged and dependents babbled and wailed all night. Today the wife and brother came up to collect gratuity pay. I paid her 12 times his base pay, a total of 29,800 piasters. She had the temerity to ask for 500 piasters more; her brother probably put her up to it. I almost gave into my emotion but stayed with policy. Major Jack Kistler and Captain James F. Richie came by today to see what all this activity was about. I'm trying to get ARVN Rangers to go into the hot area that I mentioned earlier. I doubt that they will, but I'm keeping my fingers crossed. The operation had four contacts today - no fatalities, just small stuff. They completed destroying the combat storage area, or the remains that the gunships left after their gun runs. The crews of the gunships had a ball. One time they were firing at a single VC. He was running in all directions. I think they finally got him. Overkill! This phenomenon is strange and seems to creep up on the most innocent of warriors. One minute they are kind and gentle and the next they are raving savages. I think the animal instinct takes over when the body is threatened and the brain stands down. War causes strange manifestations of behavior.

October 28, 1966 One operation came in late last night. They gave me an after action report on the VC battalion training center. It was an elaborate set-up: tunnels, mess halls, and billets. They destroyed what they could of it. Got another report today that there was another complex about six miles out. I'll send a company out there tomorrow, probably Trot Company. They plan to take packhorses with equipment. This will be the first time we use horses, the same ones we rode in the village awhile back. Or I should say tried to ride.

CHAPTER 10 AIRBORNE TRAINING

AIRBORNE TRAINING

I made a parachute jump today with the LLDB out of a CV-2. I landed right in the middle of the runway in front of the village, right where I intended. Everyone in the village ran out to see. They thought that was the weirdest thing they ever saw. We were training our counterparts and giving them the opportunity to practice jumping. Meanwhile at the end of the runway a family was mourning for another Striker who died of gunshot wounds last night. I paid her gratuity pay of 21,750 piasters.

I was invited by the province chief today to attend a ceremony at Bao Loc on November First.

October 29, 1966 Just returned from the Striker village where we were celebrating the return of two companies from successful operations. Sent another company out to check a possible company of VC. Drank a lot of rice wine with the village chief. They uncorked a huge jug of rice wine, stuck a long bamboo straw deep into it and held my nose and I drank, then the village chief, then me again back and forth. The measure was a beer can filled with water each time. You drank a can then they refilled it with water to the brim of the large jug. The only conciliation was the more you drank the weaker it got.

October 30,1966 Sent a company to Bao Loc to prepare for the parade on November 1st. Most of the day I recorded and stood by the radio. Specialist Tafoya and Sergeant Williams' Company made contact with an estimated squad of VC; killed one, wounded two, burned three ammunition storage sheds, one secondary explosion, captured one pistol, one carbine.

The horseman lost the pistol in a stream in the chaos, supposedly. One Striker wounded in the face and hands. The medical evacuation helicopter is on the way at present.

Looks like the Striker won't make it. Shot up pretty badly. All in all, a quiet day. Oh, just got a call they captured NVA documents. I'm having them translated now. Hope they are of tactical and/or strategic significance.

October 31, 1966 A CV-2, landed with gasoline for the generators and vehicles today. The pilots reminded us of what a party we missed in Nha Trang last Saturday. I told them we tried to get there but had a little VC activity at the time. Had over 300 out on operations. One company was surrounded by VC and it was a busy time. I sure wanted some of my team to go, but the timing was bad. Too bad, as the party was given in honor of Tan Rai Special Forces team. Maybe next time.

I'll be going to Bao Loc today for the ceremonies and parade tomorrow. Duc Lap had a company of Montagnards walk out on them today. They took weapons. They are considered VC once they leave the gate. I guess we are not the only camp having employment problems, probably FULRO related.

November 1, 1966 National Day The ceremony in Bao Loc kicked off at 0915 hours when the province chief finally drove up to the grand stand where 200 other guests and myself were. I then listened to several speeches in Vietnamese. Then the troops marched by. I watched my company march proudly. They surprised me. That's the first official marching they've ever done. They were picturesque with red scarves and red paint on their bayonets to symbolize battle (blood). Called camp, they have several more VC suspects in camp. Harold Coon, my new intelligence sergeant is sure doing a good job in identifying the VC infrastructure. He tenaciously follows all leads.

Attended the reception at 1700 hours with all the dignitaries. But in the early afternoon went for a swim at the French Plantation.

Stayed all night with the Navy group in Bao Loc to include Doc Siebert who probed my belly when I was shot in the lower abdomen. This time I could laugh without pain. Played bridge with Mr. Neddleton, Captain Siebert and Max. I lost.

Saigon didn't have it as quiet as we had it in Bao Loc, two separate terrorist attacks occur in the center of Saigon. In the first incident, a 75-mm recoilless rifle was fired at a crowd of civilians waiting for the start of a parade celebrating South Vietnam's National Day. In the second incident, a Vietcong grenade was thrown at a crowded bus terminal in the city's central market. At least eight people were killed in the two attacks.

November 2, 1966 Moved cross-country back to camp with the company. Was taking a shower tonight when Top Nabors told me we had 118 deserters. I had also been hearing about somebody sabotaging our ammunition in order to jam the automatic weapons. I held an alert immediately and found it wasn't so bad. However several Strikers were AWOL, probably located in the village. First thing in the morning I'll check them in as they try to sneak back in the gate. That's a good time to fire some of them. I have to cut my strength by 70 people anyhow to keep within my budget. I've been too successful recruiting. Everyone wants to join the best team.

November 3, 1966 Today was indeed a full day. I started this morning with my LLDB counterpart Thung Uy Minh, my team Sergeant, Jim Nabors, Battalion commander, K' Gee and interpreter, Mr. Minh.

We went to each company and got an accurate count of who was here and who deserted. I fired fifty people. Now I could get rid of twenty and stay within budget. I also re-organized the Security platoon. Then the airplanes started coming in. First my boss, Colonel Gillette. He was pleased with the progress and successful operations.

Colonel Gillette then said,

"There seems to be an overall slow down of VC activity in your area. What are you doing differently?"

"We are getting out on operations in a larger and more powerful force and more distant each day."

Colonel Gillette continued,

"Keep up the good work. This is one of the most impressive A-Teams in II Corps."

Then a CV-2 with much needed rice flew in. Then Captain 'Wesby' came in, in his L-19 single engine aircraft and he and I flew up over the operational area into which I am taking a company tomorrow. Looks like Charley is active in the area. Saw several hutches, a rope bridge, rice fields, and activity along the trails. Also saw three breath-taking waterfalls, one of which is supposed to be a cache' for the VC. We'll leave in the morning with a company and a reconnaissance platoon and stay five days, unless we really run into something big, in which case we may stay longer.

I wanted to jump today, we still have three parachutes still packed, but just did not have enough time for extra curricular activity. Besides General Westmoreland does not want us to jump unless it is a combat jump.

November 4, 1966 Operation Attleboro seems to be stirring up not only the VC but my troops as well. That is to say more AWOL's. The largest operation of the war is now occurring in Tay Ninh Province not far from here. Here it is, 1000 hours, and we haven't left yet. Half the company was AWOL this morning. I think we finally got it straightened out. A Montagnard lieutenant in D Company was firing everyone for every little reason. The men finally got tired of his autocratic leadership style and quit. I replaced him for the time being. We are now going to depart at 1300 hours.

I'm not sure how many people will be on the operation, in view of the circumstances. Colonel Gillette tells me there is a VC Division sized element about seven miles west of where we're going. I suppose we'll have to dig in tonight as I have reports Charley has 81mm's mortars and 75mm Recoilless weapons in that area. I hope to capture one.

Moved out at 1300 hours and continued moving until 1800 hours. The troops reluctantly shuffled through a perfect ambush site and after that precarious experience we decided to hold up for the night. As a matter of fact they would not move through the area on their own so I led the company through. I had to use the Fort Benning solution — Follow me leadership style. Unfortunately if you are the leader you have to do that when required. No action during the night.

November 5, 1966 Moved out early and traveled all day. Charley fired one sniper shot. After traveling about seven miles I got a call from camp asking me to return due to trouble with the LLDB counterparts. Darn! Rats! We were just getting in an ambush position to do Charley some harm if he should happen that way. Well, we started back, withdrew to a deserted village and set up for the night. Just before moving into the village saw a dead VC being devoured by a most beautiful tiger. He slowed down enough to glance at us then drug the body into a bush.

I remember Ned telling me he heard the Yards say Teeeger, Teeeger, and eventually he saw a Tiger out of the corner of his eye and realized what they were talking about.

Shortly after eating and checking the security and ambushes, I heard an automatic weapon open up. We all scrambled for our weapons. Then there was more firing—this time a PPSH 41. There's no mistaking the sound of that weapon—Blat-Blat-Blat. After all settled down we found out a squad of VC came strolling down the road toward my ambush. My point man got excited and set it off early. No friendly casualties. After that we got probed three times during the night, once by a buffalo. Along about 2200 hours I figured it would be "a long night" because one of my squads withdrew saying beaucoup VC, which means many, many VC. I told them to get back out there and if they withdrew again I'd shoot them myself. They stayed the rest of the night in the forward position where I wanted them. The village is apparently now a combat hamlet meaning VC controlled. There was a buffalo heard, a turnip patch, beets and rice in the open area. I guess VC come by to get food occasionally.

CHAPTER 11 COMMUNICATIONS

November 6, 1966 Sure glad to see the sunrise this morning. I doubted that I would ever see it again. I slept in a hammock last night with my Bac Xi (doctor) on one side and a Montagnard on the other. Every time Charley probed us, I'd roll out and land on the Montagnard. He didn't say anything but I bet he was sore this morning. I found out that two VC companies moved past us during the night. Early in the morning we could see them fixing breakfast, the smoke rising and they were on the reverse slope from Bao Loc's artillery. They were about two miles away. We didn't have time to go after them so I called in an air strike. As we departed we found two VC rucksacks and a Thompson Sub magazine gun and PPSH 7.62mm Russian ammunition. I guess the squad of VC we fired at left in such a hurry they left their belongings. They had civilian clothes, rice, black tire rubber for sandals, a North Vietnamese ID card and five North Vietnamese piasters on them.

The Strikers ate the buffalo they killed. There was nothing left but the bones, hoofs and hide. They didn't leave a thing. We moved all the way back to camp; traveling in a swampy area for about three hours. Got a lot of leeches on us. There's no way to avoid them. When they get full they fall off.

November 7, 1966 Started out early tackling camp problems. First challenge was 151 AWOL's. I gathered all the company commanders, LLDB, and interpreter and we got that straightened out. The truth is we'll probably keep what we have here in camp, but the AWOL's will go back to Di Linh and join the VC and become part of the VC element that is supposed to attack us. I just wonder when it will be? Our intelligence is getting better and better. We know most of the VC commanders and the units we are fighting. They are recruiting more and more now to get the rice in by the end of November. After my talk with the commanders, I talked the CV-2 pilots into dropping two of my men for a parachute operation. I had to instruct them and help them hook up. Of course I jumped along with them. Then Thung Uy Minh and I flew to Bao Loc in the two L-19s. While eating, Colonel Gillette came in so we had our conference there in Bao Loc and Thung Uy and I didn't have to fly to Buon Ma Thuot. Planned an operation for tomorrow.

November 8, 1966 The Province Chief, Colonel Sharp and his delegation came by today. Gave them a complete briefing and worked out coordination for future operations.

November 9, 1966 Flew in to Nha Trang on a CV-2 just to relax awhile and requisition a few critical items for camp. A half-hour after I got off the plane I located a case of T-bone steaks and a case of rib eye steaks. I traded a captured PPSH 41 for them. They sure will taste good. Saw and talked to a lot of old friends. Then I just relaxed watching an 8mm projector rerun at the team house, and retired early.

At the monthly B team meeting I got to visit the other commanders and team sergeants; Bill Daniel and Master Sergeant Pyburn, from Trang Phuc and Buon Ea Yang, Frank Leach and MSG West, from An Lac, Roger Segler and MSG Tatom, from Nhon Co, John H. Jackson and MSG Pylant from Lac Thien, (Pylant went to Nhon Co later), Don Sweigart, Larry Dring and SFC Mitchell, from Luong Son, Jim Evanoff and Sergeant First Class Fretwell, from Buon Blech, Bill Meder and MSG Birge from Duc Lap.

November 10, 1966 Generally requisitioned supplies and coordinated with the staff most of the day. Talked to a First Lieutenant of the Autonomous movement of the Montagnards (FULRO) at Maria Kim's bar tonight. He explained more about FULRO. He is definitely down on the Vietnamese. He is a Rhade Montagnard tribesman. Went there with Lee, Fairbanks and Jim McWilliams.

November 11, 1966 Flew from Nha Trang to Duc Lap to Buon Ma Thuot to Tan Rai today. The one company I had out on operation killed one VC and captured a PPSH 41 machine gun. Nhon Co Special Forces camp captured an NVA radio yesterday. Way to go Segler, Bob Tink and crew. Colonel Gillette has a large operation planned for us. However we have enough on our hands here. Looks like Charley is building up all around this camp. I think it's for one of two reasons: (1) he intends to overrun Bao Loc or, (2) he wants to get his rice in before the end of November. November 12, 1966

Five planes came in already and it's only 1200 hours.

The company operation came in this evening. Sergeant First Class Coon was excited as he told the story of shooting a VC point blank at five paces with an M-79 grenade launcher and capturing an AK 47 machine gun with 4 magazines. It was he or the VC; survival of the fittest and the VC lost. Do you realize how improbable hitting the guy in the head with an M-79 was? It was like a hole in one. Intelligence sources say there are quite a few VC in that area. A VC province chief turned himself in at Di Linh. That will help us break the intelligence net in that area. It was my opinion they were bandits anyhow. They were pretty clever but not as aggressive or highly motivated as the hard core VC to the north and west of us. We make contact every time we go out now. Usually four to eight miles and we're in the action. Colonel Gillette asked me to send two companies to Nhon Co on the 17th of November. He is still looking for the NVA division and expects to tackle a division command post (CP) with six companies. We're not real sure what's in that area. One way to find out is to go there.

Our team house seems luxurious and comfortable, by relative standards. We're proud of it. We all relaxed and watched a movie tonight. We invited our LLDB counterparts.

November 13, 1966 We still have 139 AWOLs. I guess they don't intend to return. They were apparently the new recruits. The only problem is they may join up with the local VC force at Di Linh and they would know the layout of this camp. I think since the ARVN draft pressure is off and they now have to get back and harvest their rice they made a mass exodus to get back home. This last Sunday was finally a day of relaxation. The Americans played softball and now the rest of the team plays poker while I sit here in my bunker, writing letters.

November 14, 1966 We have reports that there are several VC in a nearby village of Mnrong Sekang. My new people want to destroy the village. The LLDB (VN Special Forces) want to leave the village alone and the Strikers could care less except for the ones who have relatives there. The people are not in fact VC but the village is a VC safe area. Therefore it is unwise and unfair to destroy the whole village. So I decided to destroy only the houses with ammunition, weapons and VC suspected supplies in them. I know a few of the villagers and know they are pro American and pro ARVN but are under VC forced control.

Captain Clyde Sincere, who had commanded An Loc and now the MIKE (C-team reserve) force, Colonel Parmly and four other Americans were wounded up north of Pleiku. Sergeant Mitchell was killed. They have quite a bit of activity there with the North Vietnamese troops.

November 15, 1966 Settled a lot of camp problems today. I also found out the LLDB are saying one thing to us and doing another. I confronted my counterpart today about the incongruous actions, saying he had an operation out when in fact he did not. He made quick amends, excuses and said it would never happen again. Tonight I send two companies out to Mnrong Sekang to surround the village and search for VC suspects. They will be informed that any house with ammo or VC items in it will be destroyed and the inhabitants will be escorted to Bao Loc for questioning. Then we will provide medicine and civil action items for the villagers. The VC have been sleeping there every night, so I hope to capture several of them. At least this time they shouldn't be tipped off because the companies think they are going on a night training exercise in the opposite direction.

November 16, 1966 Two companies are preparing for the operation at Nhon Co Special Forces Camp. Last nights operation was uneventful. Only one suspect was found. Charlie must have been tipped off. After questioning he confirmed the fact that the VC had been in the village. We turned him loose and intend to use him as an agent. He has agreed to seek information for us and report back later. Now if the VC don't zap him because he was at our camp we may have a good agent. Fortunately the LLDB blindfolded him before bringing him into camp. While the two companies are away, I expect the VC to close in on our camp closer and closer. I think we can defend the camp with what we have left but since we won't be running too many operations Mr. Charles will get close enough to mortar us and we won't be able to do a thing about it.

November 17, 1966 A funny looking Navy airplane flew in today with a Captain from the Special Combined Intelligence Group. He's getting current intelligence and bringing maps up to date. He says down in III Corps Operation Attleboro killed 1000 VC in the past few days. We're waiting for aircraft now to go to Nhon Co for our big operation. I finally figured out Colonel Gillette's objective in such an operation. He wants us to bump up against a large VC force, like a division, so he can justify sending in American reinforcements. Seems as though American units are all tied up at the moment. Must be lots of enemy activity going on elsewhere in Vietnam.

November 18, 1966 I fired the LLBD battalion S-2, intelligence officer, today based on Coon's recommendation. He was too weak. Waved off two C-123s today as the airstrip was too muddy. They would get stuck and therefore could not shuttle troops, as is their mission.

The 61st VC battalion is about six miles away from camp now. They keep saying the plan for Tan Rai is going as scheduled. That means they will attack this camp. My agents are reporting the 61st VC battalion every day. One of the K'ho Montagnard Strikers pulled a gun on one LLDB sergeant. Now Colonel Phong, the commander at C-2 wants this man. I have since made him my Armorer and he's doing an outstanding job. I think they want to rough him up some. It's really a shame; several weeks ago, when the VC sabotaged all the automatic weapons, this Striker fixed the weapons in record time. I owe him because of that. I believe I'll keep this man right here with me.

Just one CV-2 landed. Captain Barkman left on it. Lieutenant Jones came in with food supplies only to depart again for Cam Rhan Bay for more food.

November 19, 1966 I purchased tribal skirts, loincloths, vest, knives, and spears from the Tan Rai village chief today. I'm trying to encourage an entrepreneurial attitude for the village elders. They have the crafts but no market. With little effort they could market their crafts in Bao Loc. Had a long talk with my interpreter today. I asked him to give us Vietnamese history classes. During our discussion, I noticed his resentment in being of Chinese descent. There was an underlying distrust of Chinese in his wording. The Chinese wanted to kill all the Montagnards at one time in their history. The Vietnamese and Montagnards repelled the Chinese many times over their long history.

November 20, 1966 We shuttled a company to Nhon Co on CV-2's and sent a company out on operations here southwest of camp. Heard this evening an American got killed at Nhon Co. Later found out it was SSG Jimmie C. Honely who was an outstanding Medic.

November 21, 1966 I only have four Americans on site. The others are on operation or have malaria or wounded. Consequently today I pitched in and helped as opposed to supervising. In between coordinating with Lieutenant Thai, other Strikers, and K'Gee, my Battalion Commander, I was the interior decorator for the team house. I supervised the CA/PO squad in building a bar, cleaning up, and paneling a wall. I intend to put up a display of K'ho tribesman's hand made items and costumes. And on the opposing wall I hung a display of Viet Cong captured weapons and VC flags.

The temperature is about 50 degrees Fahrenheit—it's cold.

A Vietnamese General is due to visit us tomorrow. Apparently he is the new commander of the 23rd Infantry division.

November 22, 1966 Today is a joyful day. I've been supervising the interior building of the team house. I've been teaching the CA/PO squad (9 men) wood finishing, decoration and construction. Their eyes light up with delight every time I teach them something new. Mine too, for that matter. My hand made Randall knife, that I mail ordered, came in today and also pictures of the camp and the buffalo sacrifices. I sent the pictures off to Hawaii for processing. I have lost some in the past. I can only postulate that the plane was shot down or someone liked the pictures better than I did. Lieutenant Jones sent 1000 pounds of food from Nha Trang. It was too much for our freezers—we had to send the surplus to Bao Loc. It is the simple things that one dwells on to swing from a bad mood to an outstanding mood.

The General did not show up. The local operation has had no contact yet. The Nhon Co operation has run into extensive Viet Cong non-occupied complexes. I won't get a full rundown until Master Sergeant Nabors gets back.

Specialist Ned McGonagle is on operations and doing an outstanding job. Intelligent, capable, professional and in good physical shape he is a real asset to the team. What makes Ned tick? Ned is one of those people who is happiest when left alone. Being alone provides him with the safety and solace he needs to recuperate. He does have a tendency to seek excitement, but he usually finds ways to do so without involving others. He has a wonderful laugh and dry sense of humor. He has a majestic Radio Announcers voice. Adjusting to stress is easy for Ned.

November 23, 1966

CV-2 pilots said today this place is really shaping up. They invited me to their villa in Nha Trang. They brought a turkey in for us for tomorrow, Thanksgiving. Since I only have four Americans on site I decided to wait until others return before we cook it.

November 24, 1966 Seems like there's a lot of enemy activity in all the other 'A' detachments. Maybe my company at Nhon Co is included. Luong Son's operation was under heavy fire this morning. After airstrikes and sweep through operations, the count was one CIDG shot in the leg and after walking 100 meters from their position they found eleven dead VC. They hadn't advanced beyond the 100 meters because of darkness. They expected to find others beyond that. The past few days I heard many Dust-Offs (medical evacuation helicopters). Activity is picking up. Intelligence reports indicate more activity around my area but Charley still doesn't elect to fight us. He's waiting until he has everything in his favor.

If you're wondering why we find out so much about other Special Forces camps, its because while on radio watch, usually two hours at a time, we can listen to all the activity in the entire B team to include all six A-Teams.

I have a company out southwest of camp at present with negative contact. They called in a while ago and said Sergeant Ned McGonagle had fever and shaking profusely. We all thought it could be malaria so I told them to return to camp.

We had T-bone steak tonight. It was delicious. I can remember the first three months here, no meat except buffalo and dog and then only during ceremonial occasions. These kinds of memories help us appreciate a T-bone and savor the moment. Just received a call from my company. One man stepped on a mine, which blew his foot off. I also was informed a Striker stabbed himself in the leg. Trying to find out if he did it to be evacuated. No enemy contact.

A helicopter just came in under darkness to pick up the wounded Striker. We lit up the airstrip with jeep lights and flashlights.

November 25, 1966 Left on an operation at 2000 hours, traveled until 0400 hours through very thick underbrush. The LLDB lieutenant was directing the operation, which obviously was going in circles. I had a temporary flash back to ranger school when we were exhausted and lost, going around in circles. I finally told him to stop the operation, get some sleep and get a fresh start at beginning morning nautical twilight (BMNT). BMNT is when the sun is still 17 degrees below the horizon but one can see well enough to travel also called 'false dawn'. We only traveled a straight-line distance of three miles but circuitously about ten. We set up a perimeter defense. I broke out my indigenous hammock and relaxed my weary bones.

November 26, 1966 Moved about eight miles once we were rested up. Very few signs of Viet Cong. No contact. We went through several leech forests. They wait on the trail and climb on your boots. The leeches also drop from above when they sense the body heat.

I also found out they suck the pore and introduce an anti-coagulant serum to make the blood flow. They sure leave an ugly blue mark when they get their fill and drop off. Insect repellent helps, but nothing is foolproof. The "yards" use a dust stick. They learned this technique from the Viet Cong. I remember a while back after we swept through a VC strong point. The VC left so unexpectedly that they left food and these dust sticks behind. At first we did not know what they were. It was a stick about eight inches long with a cloth wrapped around one end and tied with hemp string. Inside the cloth which formed about the size of a golf ball was the 'white dust'. You simply hit it around your boot tops, waist and wrist leaving the white powder to fight off insects and leeches. The Yards finally figured out the composition of the white powder. It is a combination of dried vegetation and pollen. It works great and the leeches hate it. I guess the leeches were nondiscriminatory and bothered the VC as well until the VC discovered the white dust stick.

November 27, 1966 Moved another nine miles today. We were hot on a fresh 16 to 20-man VC platoon trail for awhile, but lost it. Saw their campsite. Charley is staying off our trails and mining them. He's making new trails. Saw a lot of elephant signs and tracks today, killed a green pit viper. My K'ho Montagnard guard skinned him and gutted him as per my instructions. I told them I would show them how to cook and eat snake in the morning. As savage as they are supposed to be, they turned their noses up at the idea. We all laughed. Were they afraid because it was poisonous? I explained we were taught how to cook rattlesnake in ranger school. We only needed to ensure the poison sacks were stripped out.

From June 27th to Thanksgiving we've been working sixteen hours a day, seven days a week. Our typical working day begins in the predawn darkness about two hours before breakfast with calisthenics. After eating, we train the Yards in basic skills, marksmanship, hand-to-hand combat, squad movement, and first aid. We also train unconventional operations, mining, claymore mines, booby-trapping, sniping, and special weapons. After dinner we practice night-firing techniques, movement at night, light and noise discipline, and setting up night ambushes. We occasionally watch movies when they are available.

November 28, 1966 Moved to an ambush site and set up one of the most beautifully concealed, beautifully located sites I've seen. Even Mr. Charles would be proud of it. Had a whole company off the trail, camouflaged, claymores and weapons laid in, and the reconnaissance platoon out for early warning. In one direction we could see for three miles, in the other, 400 meters. It would have been deadly if a Viet Cong company would have moved into the breach. It would have been instant death. We waited. I had time to boil the snake in water but only the Americans ate it, the Yards tasted it but spit it out, and the Vietnamese would not try it.

November 29, 1966 The only thing that approached the ambush was a tiger. He came up to within 5 feet of the reconnaissance platoon, growled, and left. He showed up at about 0200 hours.

November 30, 1966 After the reconnaissance platoon told me about the tiger,

I asked, "Why didn't you shoot it"? I would have given them 2000 Piasters for the pelt.

They said, "No, the VC might hear the shots". And besides Dai Uy said, "If anyone sets the ambush off early, Dai Uy will shoot him". I forgot I said that but I guess they took it as an order. I did not mean it so harshly. Anyhow, we had excellent discipline and quietness. In fact quiet enough to entice a wild Tiger to check us out. We rolled up and moved over thirteen miles back to camp. We set up a mobile blocking force for company D on the return trip. Intelligence reported several VC bunkers built up over night (not a likely event). We were directed to check it out. The intelligence source was electronic. Probably a Mohawk aircraft flew over with an infrared camera. When we swept through the area it turned out to be elephants leaving their usual trail of straw feces and bark rubbed off the trees above our head level. The heat from the elephants must have been recorded on the infrared radar screens of the Mohawks flying overhead last night. While disappointed not to see VC, I was just as interested in observing the patterns of the elephant.

December 1, 1966 Having trouble with the LLDB again. I have word I'm going to Hawaii on Rest and Relaxation (R&R) on 13 December. We have word that the Viet Cong will mortar Tan Rai this month and will attack this camp at the end of December. I am in the process of making propaganda leaflets for this precarious period to convince the VC to turn themselves in. We are also devising tactical measures to prevent an attack.

December 2, 1966 We were expecting the CV-2s in today but looks like the late afternoon rain showers weathered them out. That means no food for the Strikers. It's been raining and cold.

December 3, 1966 Flew a visual reconnaissance (VR) today with Captain Wesby. We flew over an anti-aircraft site and looked for possible landing zones (LZ) for a future operation. Saw several new infiltration trails. Sent two platoons to Ka Tang Bla to retrieve the remainder of lumber we left after burning the ammunition storage sheds. Looks like another malaria case tonight. The LLDB Second Lieutenant has it.

December 4, 1966 Chow run finally came in, even though only one CV-2 made it in. It should sustain the Strikers for a week. No cows came in. Usually we get a load of food about twice a week. Had quite a few AWOLs again. I'm having a meeting to decide more severe punishment for the AWOLs. It is the wife, who is the boss, and tells her husband to go AWOL around payday. I'll get input from Montagnard commanders. Their perception of punishment could be different than ours.

December 5, 1966 One punishment recommended last night was, the Yard would walk around camp with a heavy rock on his head. That is a new one on me, but I guess it is humiliating to them. Anyhow I shall try it. Sam Phillips, CIA, came in today. It was his monthly visit. He enlightened us as to the events surrounding the ambush near Bao Loc. Twenty- seven ARVN were killed and twenty-three wounded, with eight missing. He further states the big picture for the VC is to cut Vietnam in half. And it just so happens that our camp is sitting in the middle of the probable takeover area. There are mountains all around us and the VC have control. All his propaganda efforts and indications lead us to believe the VC will attempt to take control of this camp. Sending four Americans out on operation means three are left in camp and to top it off a mortar attack is imminent.

Captain Owens and his Blackcats flew in today to talk, visit, and coordinate operations.

Solved quite a few team and camp problems tonight. Had a long talk with the team and counterpart. I hope we've settled our internal communication problems for the time being. Language, cultural, social and professional differences tend to be magnified and intensified at times and to add to that, emotional flare-ups widen the gap even farther. I have to stay above the emotional conflict or nothing would get accomplished. One indigenous platoon got ambushed today. Wounded two Strikers. We were able to get a slick in to med-evac them. One got it in both thighs. The other got a bullet through one cheek and had a couple of teeth knocked out. Must have had his mouth open. I'm having a recruiting poster made up of activities here in camp Tan Rai. Also my doctor is trying to get an artificial foot for one of our amputees. Our FAC pilot, Wilbanks, came in for dinner after flying a few missions for us today. The AWOLs are starting to come back. I guess harvest is over or they need money. Now, I have to decide what to do with them.

December 7, 1966 Went to the village to initiate distribution of toys for dependent children. We took pictures. It turned into mild chaos since the children were so excited. I've always thought chaos and excitement are interwoven and attitude is what determines which side of the emotion we are on. Tomorrow we'll distribute clothes to the Tan Rai villagers not the dependents. It will be more organized.

December 8, 1966 We were expecting members of the 21st Historical Detachment in today but had heavy overcast skies. They did not come. I went to the hospital for a short while this afternoon. One poor lady had a swollen and infected mammary gland. Bac Xi was going to clean and drain it. He wanted me to assist. It started to drain by itself as he put hot towels on it. He gave her codeine and antibiotics. One of my company commanders coughed up blood and had other symptoms of Tuberculosis. This is very common. Bac Xi will put him on streptomycin tablets.

December 9, 1966 Flew from Tan Rai to Buon Ma Thuot.

December 10, 1966 Saw Captain Clyde Sincere and coordinated with all staff members. He told me about his hair-raising operation. He is lucky to be alive. He was inserted from a helicopter between his men and the VC. He was engaged in a fierce fight until his men could make their way to rescue him. He tells it rather nonchalantly. I hope he writes about it some day. I ate at Johnson's with Sergeant First Class Coon, my intelligence sergeant. We laid out our strategy in building a second intelligence net.

December 11, 1966 Flew to Nha Trang saw Hemmer R. Gabriel commanding Dong Ba Thin, James B. "Jim" McWilliams, Tegote, Johnson, and others. Flew to Da Nang and tried several times to place a call to the states.

December 12, 1966 Called Heidi at 0200 hours on a Collins Single Side Band radio. It was not clear at all but I got the message through for her to meet me in Hawaii. She obviously felt intimidated by the radio procedures, waiting until I said "over" after every transmission before she could talk. She finally got the hang of it. While returning to the compound a guard stopped me and led me to believe an NVA had parachuted near the road. What kind of Bull Roar is that, I thought? I drove by the suspected area at 50 mph and clutched my Randall knife and my .32 Cal Pistol, that's all I had with me. Had dinner with Captain James E. "Jim" Kolbe, whom I knew from Germany.

CHAPTER 12 HAWAII R&R WIFE AND SON

December 13, 1966 Before leaving Da Nang I saw a U.S. Air Force jet F-4 park close to where we were standing waiting to embark on the plane leaving for Hawaii. The pilot stepped off the F-4 Phantom and shot himself accidentally in the thigh. It was one of those moments of decision. Do I go help the poor pilot who was now wallowing around on the ground, or do I hop on the airplane bound for Hawaii. Instinctively I was on my way to help the pilot when I heard a medic wagon with siren screaming toward us. I thought that was incredibly fast. The conning tower had seen the incident and reacted immediately. Thank goodness! I turned and boarded the plane for Hawaii when the medics arrived. As we left I peered out the window and the medics were putting him in the ambulance all wrapped up with one of those inflatable body contraptions. That was the first one I had seen. Later at Fort Leavenworth, Command and General Staff College in early 70's, I found out a classmate, Dr. Burton, invented that inflatable half body stabilizer.   You wrap the part to stabilize and inflate it. Ingenious! It saved many lives by preventing shock, stabilizing broken bones and bleeding bodies.

Left Da Nang at 1200 hours in flight for Hawaii. We crossed the International Dateline, and flew from daylight through darkness to daylight and stopped at Guam. We found ourselves getting very excited about our landing in the 50th state, Hawaii. Landed at the International Airport, trucked to Waikiki and got a room in the Hilton, called Heidi and Mary Lou, my sister on a real dial phone, first time in eight months.

A friend whom I had just met and I were walking down
the street when he stepped off the curb and landed
smack on one of these iron grate manhole covers. It
shrilled out with a loud bang. I dove down to take cover
and defend myself instinctively. My mind was still in
animal survival mode or combat mode. I looked up with
embarrassment once I realized I was in Hawaii and said
something stupid, like "I'm sorry, I forgot where I was."
He looked at me like I was crazy. Walked downtown to
the International marketplace where I saw a line of Hula
dancers on stage and other entertainment put on by the
island beauties. While watching the show a lady next to
me said,
"There is Cassius Clay"
The man approaching in a T-shirt and Levis said,
"No Madam, I'm Mohammed Ali."
We gathered around Ali while the hula dancers
continued on stage. I thought I would have to look up to
him, physically I mean. We are both six foot two inches
tall and as I looked him in the eye I invited him to my A
Camp in VN. He graciously declined with the remark,
"They are firing real bullets there."
Then he laughed almost diplomatically. Years later I saw
him in Washington DC and ask if he remembered the
Green Beret Captain inviting him to the A camp. He
said,
"So you was da guy?"
Then he laughed that same diplomatic laugh. I'll never
forget it. The laugh was beautiful, enormous, non-
threatening and made one feel good inside. He deserved
to be the Champ. He was the champ in my mind, even
though he declined to serve his country in uniform. He
served in his own way.

December 14, 1966 Got a rent-a-car, met, Heidi and my eighteen-month old son, Alexander, at the airport. Checked in at the Reef Hotel. Walked to the square. Alexander looked great but was very jealous of this strange man. After all, he hasn't seen me for nine months, half his life. Fine looking young man but confused after traveling thousands of miles in the past week, I guess he's wondering where home is.

December 15, 1966 Drove around Oahu.

December 16, 1966 While riding around we saw the sea park, surfers, ships, and plenty of beach. Alex got sick in the car but behaved well. He is getting reacquainted with me. Ate at Colonel's plantation. It was expensive but tasty. Everyone honors the fact I am a fighting soldier from Vietnam.

December 17, 1966 Drove around Pearl Harbor. Looked inside a submarine.

December 18, 1966 Walked Waikiki beach, packed, turned in the rent-a-car and departed at 1030 PM. It's tough to say goodbye when you are not sure if you'll ever see each other again.

December 19, 1966 Nothing to write about. This day did not exist in the life of Raymond J. Striler (crossed International Dateline).

December 20, 1966 Arrived in Da Nang at 0900 hours after stopping in Guam & Manila. Talked to my friend from Germany, Captain John Dave Blair Jr., who commanded Ashau Special Forces camp when it was overrun. Drove to Special Operations Group (SOG). C-1 is practicing extracting dead bodies. Seems as though they expeditiously buried an American on an operation. Now Department of the Army wants the body so SOG has to go back and get it, 45 days later. Upon arrival I saw the familiar site of a jet air strike several miles from the 'Rock' near Da Nang. I knew I was back in Vietnam when I literally had the crapper pulled out from under me. They have these three or six hole devices for convenience of disposing of feces. I was sitting on a six-hole'r when I heard this racket beneath me. I almost hit the dirt thinking it was incoming. Instead, it was outgoing. Mama San was pulling the half-55 gallon drum from underneath me while I was using it. To the rear about 4 meters there were three Mama-Sans burning the feces with diesel oil. They were laughing with their hand over their betel stained teeth. It was more of a 'tee hee' type laugh, as if to say,
"We dared her to do it and she did it".
I had a decision to make, finish what I came for or be embarrassed and leave. I was never one to get embarrassed over little things. I chose the former.
December 21, 1966 My 28th Birthday
At 0300 hours I flew on a KC-130 (refuel type aircraft) to Nha Trang, then took a C-123 out to Buon Ma Thuot. Ate and coordinated food supplies with Mr. Johnson, my contractor, who acted glad to see me.
December 22, 1966 Flew to Bao Loc to coordinate operations, picked up my Team Sergeant Jim Nabors and flew back to Buon Ma Thuot. Sat around and talked to team leaders and team sergeants.

December 23, 1966 This is the big 'A' detachment commanders meeting today at Buon Ma Thuot and a Christmas party on top of that. Seems like all of Buon Ma Thuot and the MAGGOTs were there. Had an intelligence report that the VC would attack the Buon Ma Thuot Special Forces camp.

December 24, 1966 Returned home today to Tan Rai, the best A camp in all of Vietnam. The new LLDB commander flew in on the same chopper with me, a lot of changes were evident and in such short time. These guys are motivated. Believe it or not there was a real holiday spirit lurking in the inner compound. A delegation plus entertainers came in from Bao Loc to entertain the troops. They stayed all night and made the routine presentations of awards to the Americans. All seems quiet. I am looking forward to the operation coming up on the 26th. We should get Charley. It will be a combined operation, six CIDG companies and two ARVN battalions, going out for about two weeks.

December 25, 1966 East Versus West Culture Differences Today was truly a day of celebration. We drank many glasses of rice wine and ate all sorts of foods from blood salad to raw ham.

About 50 Americans were here all together celebrating but also coordinating upcoming operations. The Yards planned various games and drank until their hearts were content and their heads crazy. Perhaps they over indulge because of the inevitable possibility of death or seeing the ubiquitous carnage and pain or perhaps because of the daily reminder of Communist threat. People are humble and kind. You can see this in the Christmas letters we receive. Also by the quiet personal and sentimental conversations which occur at the strangest moments with the indigenous people, both, Vietnamese and Montagnard.

Many correspondents have written about the situation over here, many wanted to, many soldiers have cried from within for want to express their feelings about the war, even as they drew their last breath of air. You senior Americans know how they feel, you young Americans can imagine. I want to speak for them and try to sum up what I feel is in the hearts of the American soldier.

First the soldier is of mixed emotions, because of the polarity of opinion by his fellow American in the United States. He is not sure that even America is backing his cause. Even though we know that the dissenters are among the vast minority, they get the publicity and seem to speak the loudest. This troubles the soldier. The fact that the soldier is a militant thinker and not a politician, he cannot understand the procrastination from all-out tactics, to win. This troubles him. The erroneous reporting and generalizations which he reads in the magazines and newspapers disturbs him. One that I recall is written as fact that every American in South Vietnam is getting seven pounds of food daily to include fresh milk and meat. Who could be so naive as to believe this, or who could be so naive as to print this?

The war is always our concern. We would all like to turn our heads and say, "That's miles away, and on another continent." It would give us temporary ease of conscience. However, thanks to you people who have reminded us over the Christmas holidays that we are not fighting alone and we are special and appreciated.

I would like to share one letter from many received here at Tan Rai Special Forces camp from a nearby village. It is this letter, support, and encouragement that make us proud to serve America in a foreign land and do the job we came here to do.

I would venture to say that even though this message is not transmitted but once or twice a year, that it is representative of how the people of Vietnam feel; and we often forget it in the heat of battle.

Christmas letter from a teenage student in Bao Loc to the men of Special Forces at Tan Rai

Bao Loc, (dated) December 22nd 1966

> *My dear,*
>
> *Here it is Christmas again and you are still in this war and poor nation.*
>
> *I think that you are sad because your homesickness. What word, I must say to you, my dear but I know there is a respect of mine for you. A soldier with vigor on the arms and power in the heart.*
>
> *You left your lovely fatherland, parents, friends, darling and the others in order to win this fierce battlefield and to defend the free world against communists.*
>
> *I believe that you realize our self-defense war. Our blood has been shedding, so I take revenge upon the enemies.*
>
> *Both of us want to live a peaceful life.*
>
> *Let's forget the war. God will come but anyway my dear. I just want you to know that we're thinking of you on Christmas day.*
>
> *I send you my love and hope that you'll have a merry Christmas, and a very happy New Year.*
>
> *Always affectionately yours. Tupuh Dinh Le Ion Nong Lam Duc, Bao Loc.*

(Note: A hand drawn picture of three pine trees, stars, a moon, two birds, and a pathway and a boy with girl walking and holding hands accompanied the letter.)

I say on behalf of the Americans Thank You for allowing us the honor. Americans are among the most helpful and generous in the world. I realize some have to go with a minimum to support the cause in which they believe. It's a great sacrifice. Americans have sacrificed greatly for what they believe in. You have to answer the question: "Is it worth it?"
I answer for my men,
"It is, for the members of Tan Rai Special Forces camp".

SECTION FIVE: JOINT OPERATIONS

CHAPTER 13 VIETNAMIZATION AND JOINT OPERATIONS

December 26, 1966 Got ready for the operation today, departed at 1600 hours. Linked up with Nhon Co (two companies) and moved under darkness to B' Dru. Stayed all night.

I scribbled this out before the operation:

Here on another corner of the world, there is a dormant people who think and act so differently from Crystalites (my hometown) that it is inexplicable. All the books and conversation in the world could not possibly convey the true comparison. Experiencing is the only way possible to believe it, a fable for which we Missourians are famous. Said another way, "Show me."

Life is cheap here because we are in a war zone, but truly it is not: life and freedom are more precious to these Asians than to any American.

December 28, 1966 Nhon Co Special Forces company got mortared tonight about 400 meters from our campsite. I called in artillery on Charley. He vanished — no casualties.

December 29, 1966 I held in a blocking position area all day while other companies tried to scare something our way. No activity.

December 30, 1966 Came off operation today at 0900 hours. Went to Bao Loc to a ceremony to receive a Vietnamese Cross of Gallantry Silver award for a previous action in July. General Vinh Loc was in such a hurry he canceled the awards portion of the festivities so I guess I have to wait a few weeks — oh, well. I didn't mind as I was more interested in getting my troops back and getting something to eat than receiving the heroism award.

After we all drank too much in Bao Loc, we drove across no-man's land to Tan Rai in one jeep. I wanted to stop in Tan Phat and stay all night but my counterpart, Dai Úy (recently promoted) Minh, did not want to. I wonder if he knew that the VC were in the village?

Later, received intelligence that 100 VC were in Tan Phat, the little village just south of Tan Rai, when we drove through this evening — and I was planning on staying all night there. I'm glad my counterpart talked me out of it. The VC abducted one of my agents — a 13-year-old girl.

December 31, 1966 Majors Wilson, Jones, Alkinson, and Jack Kistler plus Colonel Sharp were in today coordinating the upcoming operation. Three Huey 1B's flew in so I made a reconnaissance of the operational area.

Tonight we drank, sang, and watched TV movies. Happy New Year such as it is.

January 1, 1967 Happy New Year! 1967

I had the honor of promoting and pinning Captain bars on my executive officer, Chet Jones yesterday and just as quickly his replacement came in today. Jones is reassigned to B-23. I hate to lose him. With everyone leaving it reminds me how little time I myself have left before I return to the USA. I am attempting to get circuitous travel and return to the States via India, Greece and Europe rather than across the pacific. I do not have my orders yet but should receive them any day. We are all thankful for having a good Christmas and New Years holiday in spite of the fact we are away from our loved ones. We are alive, not maimed, well-fed and healthy for what else could one ask? Boy, do I miss my family. It is so unbearable at times. The only relief is to constantly keep busy. I constantly strategize how I am going to maintain this camp as the best A Camp in Vietnam and at the same time outwit my foe.

January 2, 1967 Re-Culturing and Transition Back To The States

Indeed this has been a long day. The six CIDG companies were finally heli-lifted to the alternate-landing zone. The weather would not allow them to go into the original landing zone. One chopper crashed, one CIDG was injured in the head with serious lacerations from the blade of the helicopter and died one hour later. Shortly after everyone left, Lieutenant General Heintges flew in. He has been here before. He is General Westmoreland's deputy. I gave him a quick briefing, and then he wanted to fly my operational area. We spent 15 minutes flying and returned. His showing up should have told me that my AO (Area of Operations) was hot with VC activity.

January 3, 1967

The VC mortared the company out on operations. Fifteen Strikers were wounded. We evacuated them today, mostly superficial shrapnel wounds. My people found many traces of Charley and encountered four contacts. Just heard another Striker was wounded. I can't get the med-evac in until morning due to weather and availability of aircraft. A Striker ran up to me tonight and reported that a platoon of VC was spotted just outside the wire. It was just before dusk. He pointed them out to me and we put mortar fire on them. We'll do body damage in the morning. I expect that we will get mortared tonight. I called an alert and inspected all the fighting positions. I passed lots of radio traffic today because of all the VC activity around camp.

January 4, 1967 The operation had three contacts today, one CIDG wounded. Having continual challenges getting med-evacs in because the weather is so soupy. Can hardly see a damn thing. The area where we pumped the mortars into netted negative enemy but there were traces of ripped uniforms.

January 5, 1967 Helicopter Security Operation
The operation returned, therefore, leaving no security on the helicopter that crashed a few days ago. I received word from Colonel Gillette on the single side band radio to take an element out and secure the helicopter black box.

I took an under-strength company out at 1600 hours. We forced marched until 1900 hours and at about the half way, the point element, two Strikers, sat down and would not move. It was dark and they were approaching a likely ambush site. I quickly advanced to their position and gave them the confidence to continue. I then led them through the danger spot. Later, I heard it had to do with tribal territorial boundaries. They had never been there before on operations and that was their cousins territory – their VC cousins. That is why they would not advance forward. I had to do what they taught me at Fort Benning, lead by example. I took Point Man through the heart of the ambush site. Always something new to learn.

January 6, 1967 We moved out at 0730 hours. About an hour later we heard Charley shooting AK 56 automatic rifles attempting to draw us away from the chopper. We arrived at the chopper. I left a security element there and we moved up in Mr. Charles territory and saw several bivouac areas and a grapefruit freshly eaten half way. We figured he was 30 minutes ahead of us. We were right on his tail. He left in a hurry. We kept pursuing.

January 7, 1967 We tried but could not muster up any more contacts with Charley. He knows this area better than we do. He kept evading. A helicopter crew came in and got the black boxes. Mission accomplished, we then returned about nine miles to camp. There were no traces of Charley after we left the bivouac area. Charley is a worthy guerrilla opponent in this province. He only makes contact when he knows he'll get the best of the situation.

January 8, 1967 The L-19 pilot, Major Marlow asked me to show him where the VC battalion holding area was that we came up against last week. We flew over at tree top level. Then the Bombers were brought in. From then on it was 30 minutes of hell for Charley and 30 minutes of excitement for me. After it was all over, Napalm, 20 mm, 500 lb. bombs, and Bouncing Betties, we made an assessment and found temporary shelters that we did not know were there. Marlow was 100% on target.

January 9, 1967 Wrote deserving awards for my team members today. It is such an honor to be able to recognize their bravery. One company of VC was reported south of the camp about one mile away.

January 10, 1967

I am on a clean up kick now. I cleaned up the team house and tomorrow I will have a detail clean up the inner perimeter. If a commander does not stay on top of the cleanliness of the camp it really slides as everyone considers his job more important. But if you consider organization and ease of decision under a clean and organized operation-cleanliness should come close to first. One company departed for an operation. They left at 0800 hours and tomorrow I send out a medical/ psychological operation patrol.

Bao Loc called and asked me to brief a "bird colonel" (Full Colonel) tomorrow. That gives me assurance that they are impressed with our operation. Colonel Gillette leaves in five days. I hate to see him go! It won't be long and I'm out of here as well, March 67.

CHAPTER 14 DRINKING RICE WINE WITH THE ENEMY

What started out to be a customary visit with the village chief turned out to be an unusual event. There he was sitting cross-legged with a frown on his non-committal but inquisitive face. His anxiety seemed to rise when he saw me. The village chief introduced this distinguished guest as his boss.

"Dai Uy this is my boss,"

The chief said, as we dropped in on them unexpectedly. I was confused because I thought I was the boss, the senior-ranking official. Now, I hear the chief say, "This guy is my boss."

What is going on? I knew something was amiss. Immediately, I realized this was the Viet Cong Commander in my area of operations collecting taxes and gathering intelligence. Here is my opponent on the battlefield and I was face to face with him in this social environment drinking wine. I assessed his appearance. His face was stern with high cheekbones. His maxillary muscles methodically crunching, synchronous with his heartbeat. His eyes were deep in the sockets but wise looking. I felt I knew him immediately. One could see the experience and grief meshed together. The deep dark scar on his cheek, jaw and neck added to his mystical warrior image. I expected him to be bigger and more domineering after all of the stories of savagery, cruelty and truculence that I heard. He was not the giant I expected now that he was in my presence. What do you do when you meet your enemy eye to eye? I left my M-16 "black gun" in the jeep and only had a .32 caliber pistol in the small of my back.

He appeared unarmed but I knew his bodyguards were nearby. I'm equally sure he had a pistol beneath his black pajamas.

I whispered to Orona,

"This is a moment that you will tell your grandkids about; that's the enemy in cold blood".

I don't remember talking about anything in particular except the school and fishpond we had built for the village people. I made a conscious decision to get the hell out of there ASAP. As we left the hutch, I looked over my shoulder and there were two bodyguards standing nearby with PPSH-41'S. In retrospect, we did the prudent thing undoubtedly saving our lives to fight another day.

Sp5 Chuck Orona young, good looking, tall, smart, always wanting to learn something new is slow talking, fun loving and always tricking someone. Chuck is the absolute best medic in Special Forces. Not only skilled in medical training but cross-trained in all skills of an A team especially a good fighter.

January 11, 1967 The Fifth Special Forces Group historical team visited us today. They consist of a historian, public information expert, and a psychologist. Captain Bartman is the OIC (Officer in charge). They were enjoyable to talk with and I'm sure they thought we were crazy. I had a CA/PO patrol out and when Colonel Sharp, Colonel Kirk, and Colonel White from Bao Loc and the Inspector General (IG) visited I gave them a quick briefing. Later we flew to Mnrong Sekang where the patrol was operating. Bac Xi Orona had just finished distributing toys and medicine. He had a psychological tape playing at the time we arrived. Looks like Tan Rai may be featured in the Green Beret magazine. An agent reported today that the air strike three days ago was devastating. It destroyed rice and dispersed the VC in the area. Probably killed a few and wounded several.

January 12, 1967 Colonel Sharp visited today to discuss operations. Sergeant Templar flown in by Captain Wilbanks picked up 20,000 VN piasters for recruiting. Captain Chet Jones and his turtle, Lieutenant Bruch, returned. Jones leaves tomorrow for Hong Kong for R & R (Rest and Recuperation).

By the way, when we go on operations all essential elements of information such as who, what, where, when, why and how are kept secret until the final decision to move out. That is when the direction is told to the leaders of the troops. Sometime we depart in one direction then circle around and go the opposite direction in order to confuse the enemy. No one knows the ultimate objective until the Green Beret announces it.

January 13, 1967 Increased activity in a nearby village of Mnrong Sekang caused me to go to Bao Loc today and talk to Colonel Sharp about relocating the Montagnards of that village. They have been supporting the VC extensively. I had dinner there and chatted with all the MACV team. We discussed future operations.

January 14, 1967 My boss, Colonel Gillette, came by today to say good-bye. He is departing for the states shortly. I hate to see him go. He has done a spectacular job and supported every decision I made. We had a few beers with the LLDB at the village today. An operation went out at midnight. The weather has been terribly foggy, visibility about 50 meters and ceiling 30 meters. That limits incoming aircraft and puts us in a bind for re-supply.

January 15, 1967 The operation rounded up 70 VC suspects. They are the people in and around Mnrong Sekang. I turned them over to province in hopes province may discover discrepancies on their ID cards. The S-5, Captain Jack, flew in today in a Swiss Pilatus Porter (Air VN) airplane and delivered about 500 lbs. of Civil Affairs/Psychological Operations items, which simply means more leaflets.

Two new captains were along for the ride. I'll venture to say one will be my replacement.

January 16, 1967 I constructed a Bar-B-Que pit in the team house. Wrote recommendations for valor ribbons for Orona and Jones. The operation returned today. The cold weather extreme of the central highlands has plagued us lately. It is in the 40's. Apparently high winds have hit all of Vietnam. Flying is at a minimum as the winds gust up to 50 or 60 knots.

January 17, 1967 I'm learning more and more about the VC due to Sergeant First Class Coon's excellent intelligence networks. We believe now that every time an operation goes out one runner goes to the village and delivers the plan. Then the VC sympathizers build a fire on the side of camp in which the direction of the operation goes. To counter this, first of all we have stopped all movement between 1900 hours and 0530 hours outside the gate. We initially go one direction out the gate then reverse direction and only the American Green Beret knows where the final objective is. A guard just fired three rounds. As I rushed over I found out one Striker was trying to get out the gate. Could he be a spy? We'll watch him closely.

Of the 70 VC suspects we sent to Bao Loc on the 15th, fifteen were evidenced as handling weapons. Five of them were friendly agents from Bao Loc or double agents. That has yet to be determined.

January 18, 1967 I bartered with the village chief on items to take home with me, such as cross bows, costumes, a woven carpet and bracelets. We were audited today and were over 15,000 Vietnam Piasters. That is pretty good. Captain Wesby dropped by and Sergeant Roger Templar returned to camp successfully from his recruiting campaign.

January 19, 1967 Packed my hold baggage today. I'm reminded that I myself have to sit at the couth table soon. Probably next week I should start. The couth table is set properly with napkins, mess kit, utensils and tablecloth. The philosophy is that the short timers sit at this table in the team room and mind their manners. No cussing, no reaching, or talking out of turn, no talking while chewing, if they screw up they put 5 cents to the coffers. I try to point out that when they return to the US, "You will be different and your loved ones will treat you differently. It will be impossible to explain all that has happened to you. It is better to keep it inside until the time is right. You will know when that is so. After all your loved ones have not been exposed to danger and have not changed. They stayed at home doing the same thing. It is us, who have changed. We have seen war, the ugly side of it, the spilled blood, the broken and maimed limbs, the amputees, and the twisted bodies. Don't be surprised at how loved ones react to you. Just keep in mind they are the same and be empathetic to them while at the same time know yourself."

January 20, 1967 Waited all day for a plane. I guess Buon Ma Thuot was weathered in. Played pinochle tonight. My team members woke me up and had a message telling me my extension was approved. They were just joking of course. I hope.

January 21, 1967 I rode on a food run CV-2 to Nha Trang. Jones and Siegler just got back from Hong Kong and we watched the 'Lost Command'. Saw Lieutenant Colonel Ludwig Faistenhammer, Truffa, Aiken and others. I continue to be impressed with Colonel Faistenhammer, I remember when we were cross-country skiing in Germany and stopped in this guest house.
He surprised the waitress with his perfect Bavarian language.

We all laughed at how surprised she was. I also remember at the officers club at Bad Tölz, Germany, we were in our 'dress blues' on New Year's eve when Ludwig hoisted the commander, Colonel Jerry Sage, on his shoulders and carried him around singing to the 'umpa umpa' German music. Colonel Sage is known for the movie they made of him called "The great Escape." Colonel Faistenhammer is a real professional and I, for one, am glad that he volunteered for Special Forces over here. He understands this kind of war. We had a long talk. He wanted to know how it was at the A detachment level. Later I heard how his tumultuous relationship with Colonel Kelly turned out. He apparently was always playing tricks on Colonel Kelly. It was purported that Faistenhammer exited Kelly's office, dropped his drawers and mooned Kelly saying, "If you want my ass get it now because I'm out of here". That came from several sources so I give it a B2 for credibility.

January 22, 1967 Commanders conference here in Nha Trang today. Westmoreland and all the brass around. Tried getting things done, but it was hopeless, everyone was tied up with the conference.

January 23, 1967 Picked up furniture for the team house. Laid on a CV-2 to take supplies and furniture back to camp. Got everything accomplished with one exception, my orders. They haven't come in yet. Rats!

January 24, 1967 Took the 511 flight to Buon Ma Thuot, a C-123. Surprisingly the whole B-team has changed. I did not recognize anyone. Colonel Gillette is gone and seems like everyone else as well. The new staff is experiencing the same challenges we experienced back in May when we were new. They are trying to absorb all that massive information in a short time.

January 25, 1967 Checked all my paperwork. The bog down seems to be right here in Buon Ma Thuot. It's a shame an A detachment commander has to check constantly on small items like this. Actually they are not small items to the individual but they are handled in a small way, especially with this "new regime", they have not been around long enough to know the ropes. Makes me want to get out of here sooner.

Flew to Tan Rai on a CV-2 that Andy diverted for us. Andy is the consummate supply sergeant. He can make it happen anytime, anyplace, anyhow. The plane was full of gas, oil and diesel fuel. Good to get back to camp where something is always happening. A Catholic Chaplain was there visiting. He said mass at the Tan Rai village at 1700 hours. McGonagle, Coon, and myself attended.

January 26, 1967 Father McDinnell said Mass again at 0700 hours. The VC were sniping at the villagers of Tan Rai. SFC Coon went to check it out and found ten VC collecting taxes at the Frenchman's house. The Frenchman said that was his local security. I flew to Bao Loc today. John Curtis came back with me. He is the Officer in Charge or the head honcho for civil affairs. Major Grany and I talked about a rural development program for Mnrong Sekang.

January 27, 1967 Another day, another Mass conducted by Father McDinnell. A CV-2 came in after attempting to land several times. He finally broke through the early morning ground fog. The normal flight pattern is to come in high and drop fast, make one turn and down on the runway to avoid ground fire. I flew to Bao Loc to spend the day coordinating the relocation of Mnrong Sekang. Father McDinnell flew on to Nha Trang.

January 28, 1967 Today was a day of planning and deciding what Charley is up to. I went to Bao Loc to talk to Colonel Sharp and two other individuals about a significantly large VC meeting; believed to be provincial level. They want us to snatch up the big wheels at this meeting. Tomorrow I fly reconnaissance with one of district's spy agents, to see if he knows what he is talking about. A company-sized operation is going out tonight. Tomorrow looks like a busy day.

January 29, 1967 Colonel John E. Rossi came in today with Colonel and Madam Phong. Rossi, Colonel Patch's replacement, is the C detachment commander and Phong is his counterpart at Pleiku. I gave them a quick tour and a briefing. Then I changed to civilian attire and went on an air reconnaissance in an Air Vietnam Pilatus Porter aircraft. It looks like a square kite in flight. The VC agent was along to show the location. He confirmed everything and left little doubt in my mind that he knew the territory and knew what he was talking about. We picked up Colonel Sharp, flew to Buon Ma Thuot, talked to Colonel Johnson, flew to Nha Trang, and talked to General Norton, who agreed to commit two battalions of the 101st Airborne. We adjourned. I went to the Special Forces compound, talked to Colonel 'Blackjack' Kelly about the operation and he wanted to deploy Special Forces on one side of the operation in a parachute landing operation. Meetings tomorrow to resolve everything and decide on tactics.

January 30, 1967 At 0800 hours I gave all the intelligence reports to Major Robert (Bob) A. Kvederas Operations Officer, one fine officer, then went to Field Forces VI with Colonel Kelly to a meeting with General Norton, General Matheson (101st Airborne) and about 20 other colonels. Resolved to kick off the operation on February 1st after a B-52 strikes at 0900 hours. The force will be composed of two battalions airlifted in Chinook helicopters from the 101st Airborne Division and one battalion of II Corps Mike Force jumping in. Captain Lee Wilson commands the Mike Force. Looks like an interesting operation. There should be about five VC companies or about four hundred VC in the immediate area and more out and around. After leaving Nha Trang, I flew to Buon Ma Thuot, talked to my new boss Major Jones who replaced Gillette and then flew back to Tan Rai. My new counterpart reported into camp today. Lieutenant Tho Truong Nguyen. He seems like an experienced trooper. January 31, 1967 Gave the team a rundown of what was happening. Issued an operations order then packed for the operation, and flew off with SFC Coon and Sergeant Templar to Phan Rang. I spared them of my 'Atilla The Hun' Leadership Principles lecture. They could sense that I was in a hurry. We made one final reconnaissance on the way out. At Phan Rang, Headquarters of the 101st airborne, I saw Captains Dick Maglan, Earnest "Wayne" Dill and Pete Kiefer. The meetings started early and went through the course of the evening. We were flown in a wing formation to Phan Thiet (staging area) where we slept on the South China Sea Beach. What irony! People pay hundreds of dollars to visit beach areas like this and here we are, free.

February 1, 1967 Our part of the operation kicked off at 0900 hours. We flew in formation to the target area of D'tan Ja Rang. I flew with Colonel Collins, the commander of the 1/327th Airborne Battalion. Only one contact on LZ Shirley. Colonel Vance and Captain Zockey were wounded. One CH-47 Chinook crashed with 17 wounded. They will be brought into Tan Rai initially for quick medical triage then evaluated and flown accordingly. I flew the area most of the day pointing out terrain to Colonel Collins. General Matheson visited.

February 2, 1967 Flew area several times in the 'command and control chopper'. One more chopper shot at and three were wounded. When I returned to camp at 1500 hours Colonel Johnson and Colonel Rossi were here to greet me. Also several chopper crews. Sergeant Bobby Clark and Sergeant Major Jim Nabors returned today from their operation around Nhon Co Special Forces Camp. The CASS man flew the area again with the VC agent. The agent says the meeting was called off on the 31st. Also the location of the meeting changed. I surmised the VC changed it because of all the aircraft activity and the flashes from the cameras on the Mohawk the night before we kicked off the operation. I would have been skittish also.

February 3, 1967 Another long day. We are running a re-supply point here at Tan Rai, medical evacuation holding area, and a VIP briefing area. This morning the Mike Force commanded by Lee Wilson, a fine commander, ran into an ambush and a booby trap, probably a crudely rigged artillery 105 round. It killed three Americans. As we lifted them onto the airplane I recognized Lieutenant Casimir Niespodziany, a colleague from the 10th Special Forces in Germany. He had holes all over him. He went fast.

The operation is finding a lot of VC tunnels, rice and documents. Helicopters are being shot at repeatedly. We had several wounded, some serious. I guess the double agent warned the VC to stay clear of the area.

February 4, 1967 Its 0200 hours and we just got mortared, three 60 mm rounds. We fired fourteen rounds in defense and sent out two squads. Looks like Charley is after the helicopters sitting out on my runway. The choppers, two 'gunshots' and two 'slicks', certainly make a good target. No reported casualties yet. The mortars hit around the west wall and around the choppers. Colonel Johnson, Major 'Pappy' Lamar, and four pilot crews stayed here the last two nights to assist in command and control of the operations. Oink squealed his customary warning when he heard the incoming but the visitors forgot about that part of the briefing we give everyone staying in camp. I put all Americans underground anyway.

The operation terminated today. It was successful. It was a relief when the last chopper lifted off. One chopper lost power and landed outside the wire (outer perimeter). We had security around it in ten minutes. One of my own yards tossed a grenade into a bunker tonight. No one was inside when it went off. He is in jail now, bleeding profusely. Apparently the Strikers worked him over pretty good. Colonel Rossi wanted to discuss why I jumped channels and didn't inform my counterparts of what was happening. I told him I did not have time and thought it would be more expeditious if I went right to higher headquarters. He shrugged as if to say OK. One of our agents said the VC commander in this area was killed during the B-52 bombing.

February 5, 1967 It is relatively quiet today. Captain Chuck Miller, my turtle, left here for Ben Hoi to finalize his duties as Summary Counts Officer for Sergeant Duncan. That delays my departure as I'll have to wait for his return, break him in, sign over property, get my orders, then I'm on my way to the states. I'll take circuitous travel ergo go westward over the Middle East. Then again I might just go straight eastward to Fort Bragg, North Carolina, where Heidi and Alexander are. Time will tell. I will be ready for either eventuality. I can't wait to get on that plane. Where are my Orders?

February 6, 1967 I finally sat myself at the 'couth' table again. It is hilarious trying to say, "please" to a fellow Special Forces colleague and even funnier when he says, "you're welcome." Our new executive officer, Lieutenant Barry Bruch, left for Buon Ma Thuot today to take the monthly pay roll report back. For a Lieutenant he is really mature and has experience. That is the only way Lieutenants get assigned to SF, if they have experience.

Bac Xi Orona called last night to notify me my orders were in. My anxiety could hardly be contained while I waited to hear where I would be assigned.

He said,

"In my haste to get you the information Dai Uy, I forgot were you were being assigned."

Maybe he did not want to be the one to tell me, for some reason. Now my suspicion and anxiety were battling each other. Where would it be?

VC activity has slowed down prior to the lunar New Year, TET February 9th. I expect the VC will try for one victory prior to TET. We are taking extra precaution. I understand the VC have asked for a seven-day truce. South Vietnamese Officials asked for four days. At any rate, it is a perfunctory gesture on both sides, as I don't believe operations will slow down. The operation, Gatling Two, is finding a lot of food caches' and tunnels.

By the way this is what I think about the Couth table:
The stages I went through this year can best be described
as, 1) wondering if I would be fit for the job and
improving my physical and mental condition. I prepared
myself mentally by reading voraciously about the
oriental mind. I read The Baghavad Gita, Upanishads,
Buddha and General Giap's diary in order to understand
the Asian mind and culture. I read Siddhartha by
Hermann Hesse, which left a lasting impression on me. I
read Edwin Reischauer and Street without Joy. Trying to
make sense out of all of this was mind boggling for this
young man who had roots in Crystal City, Missouri. 2) I
did hundreds of push-ups, walked daily on my hands
and ran 5 miles daily. 3) I practiced using my left hand,
arm, eye, and leg just in the tragic event that something
might happen to my dominant extremity.
4) During the second phase I evolved into an instinctual
animal creature, one with inexplicably natural keenly
honed survival skills. The animal in me turned out to be
more dominant than the intellect at times and far more
reactive. I had to constantly remind myself to analyze
and synthesize and add a bit of dignity and levity during
this animalistic condition. When I was able to laugh, I
was the conduit of emotion for everyone else. I tried to
keep in mind that I was the catalyst, and that if I could
cause my team members to laugh, they would
automatically release their excess fear, and tension that
seemed inevitably present during battles.

I felt at times I was in touch with my sixth sense. This magic was passed down to me by my great, great grandfather who immigrated to the USA in 1847, my father, Hugo, who could really laugh existentially, and my mother, Mary Jane, who always seemed to be sensitive to everyone's needs. I always knew just before the enemy fired their weapons. It proved to be an invaluable survival skill and saved my life on several occasions. This uncanny sense of survival, this God given instinct seemed to happen to most of the men who were continuously on operations.

The third and last phase that occurred just before I returned to the USA, was one of being re-cultured. There was a conscious effort to become more aware of others and push the animal survival instinct inside under control of the intellect prior to returning to the States. This is why I invented the couth table.

February 7, 1967 Ned McGonagle was promoted to E-5. He was proud, as we were of him. He is so deserving, being so young, so talented and so humble. And on top of that he is an excellent leader of his company when in combat. We are getting ready for Charley to attack us. It has to be tonight or after TET. I registered the 4.2-inch mortar and broke a base plate. Luckily we have an extra. Registering procedure is locating a unit precisely in its field location from hearing what they see while you launch rounds. We also registered 80 mm, 60 mm's, two 81's and a 57-mm recoilless rifle. We will send an operation out tonight around camp to set up an ambush and that should secure us for TET.

About 1600 hours the company commanders came over and invited the Americans to drink with them. That lasted all evening. The dialogue was much like what I read in Attila the Hun.

February 8, 1967 This is New Year's Eve on the lunar calendar. The Strikers were given half a day off plus the next three days. We were invited to another party by the LLDB. The Air Force pilots, Wesby and Wilbanks came in from Bao Loc and joined us. We ended the party by commissioning the village chief to bring three horses out. We rode them. They are real small and our feet almost drug on the ground. Had a ball.

The VC put up an archway on highway 20 during TET and painted a sign on it.

"All travel is free. No taxes during TET."

As I was preparing my water for a shower I noticed ARVN and VC firing tracers all along highway 20. You can tell the difference; the red tracers are ARVN and the green tracers are VC.

Colonel Sharp visited us awhile yesterday. He is always amazed at the progress here at Tan Rai. His main concern is safety of the convoys coming up highway 20 and the lack of security at district headquarters in Bao Loc. His concern is; he has no reserves. I reckon he is trying to figure out how to use us in case of emergency.

CHAPTER 15 TET FEBUARY 9TH

February 9, 1967 The Historical Team visited today. We had a three-hour discussion (taped) on camp activities, Operation Gatling I, and history of the camp.

Could it be we are winning the war? We received a message today indicating the Viet Cong were releasing American prisoners and to be on the lookout for them. An American comedian/magician visited us tonight. We took him to the village, and drank rice wine. The chief gave him a tribal bracelet, which absolutely delighted him. Then he put on a show for us after which he gave me a three dimensional picture of Jesus. I hung it on the team house wall above the bar so everybody could see it.

February 10, 1967 Major Jones visited today. Had an alert tonight, which means I get everyone to battle stations and have a head count. Because of TET I have only 137 troopers in camp. That is considerably low. I typically would like 200 Strikers at this stage of our development but considering it is TET holiday, I can't complain knowing traditionally everyone migrates home. In theory this should pertain to the VC and NVA. Then they could leave a force behind and surprise weaker forces. I suspect TET celebration has a higher priority than camp defense. I sent the three advisors of company A, C, and Reconnaissance platoon to get the company commanders and platoon leaders and put them on restriction for seven days. This means they are restricted to the camp environs and can only go to the village when allowed. That insures me of control for this up coming tumultuous period.

February 11, 1967 Flew to Bao Loc to catch a ride to Buon Ma Thuot. Flew to Buon Ma Thuot in a Pilatus Porter aircraft with Sergeant Templar via Gia Nhia. We talked about his plans to apply for Officer Candidate School. I believe he will be a fine officer. I gave him words of encouragement and told him I would give him the highest recommendation.

February 12, 1967 Mailed my hold baggage back to the States. Put in all my paperwork for my departure and coordinated with other staff members. Topped the day off at the club where everyone gathered for Lieutenant Manning's promotion party. Talked with Major Benjamin.

February 13, 1967 Finally got a few things accomplished, as the Vietnamese and Americans went back to work after the long TET holiday period. Flew back to camp today with Captain Wilbanks who is flying out of DaLat now. Five minutes after I returned; Colonel Simpson and a Colonel S-2 visited. I gave them a briefing, then settled down to a Bar-B-Q beef plate.

Major Du, commander of the Special Forces B Team at Buon Ma Thuot, was excited to show me orders with my name on it for a Cross of Gallantry with Silver Star today. He will reproduce copies, have it translated and present it to me next week. I was pleasantly surprised and delighted.

February 14, 1967 It is 0230 hours. I'm on guard and all is quiet. Inventoried equipment with my replacement, Captain Chuck Miller, yesterday in preparation for him to sign for and take command of Tan Rai Special Forces Camp, best A-Team in Vietnam.

Painted azimuth markings on the 81-mm mortar pit today so as to expedite finding the azimuth when firing at night. Actually this was General Heintge's idea that he passed on to me during his last visit. Chuck Miller left to sign for the camp property. Got a television in today but looks like we are in the wrong topographical area. We can't get a thing.

February 15, 1967 The operation has had negative contact. Saw lots of trails and traces of movement, but no Charley. I believe Charley moved north on the first of January and hasn't returned to this province yet. When he does I imagine he'll come in strength, replenished and ready to fight.

February 16, 1967 VC activity is picking up a little. I guess they are returning to the operational area after the TET holiday. I heard they would take seven days and they did. Operationally, I guess everything will get back to normal. A few days ago Charley snuck into the helipad at Nha Trang and destroyed eight choppers and blew the gate down.

We received two starlight scopes for the M-16 rifle today. They light up the battlefield at night. We can see VC but they cannot see us. We experimented and zeroed in on them tonight. These scopes are dynamite and should change the whole balance of power at Tan Rai. Now I have control of the night.

February 17, 1967 The company on operation made contact with Charley today. Captured one shotgun. Called in an air strike and will check out the strike zone at first light.

February 18, 1967 Flew to Bao Loc just south of camp today, was actually trying to get to Nha Trang, SF headquarters. No aircraft available, so I went to Saigon on the mail run. As I walked toward the terminal Captain Joe Mann drove up. I stayed at his villa. I knew Joe in Germany. I especially liked the smell of the clean white sheets on the beds and bacon and eggs for breakfast.

February 19, 1967 Flew out of Saigon from 3rd Corps Air Defense Group at 0700 hours. Now it's a C-123 and all the formalities of the Air Force, manifest and time schedules. Before, one could just hop on the airplane and go. Now its paperwork; Who are you? When are you going? Where are you going? It is a real hassle.

February 20, 1967 The company on operations is having success. They are using the starlight scope extensively. Bobby Clark told me about observing a small VC unit herding elephants down the trail carrying equipment at night. Bobby obviously played havoc with them, and they had no idea where the action was coming from.

February 21, 1967 Just waited around headquarters to get my orders. Finally at 2000 hours Lieutenant Chavez, personnel officer, got through to Washington. They informed me I was going to Fort Huachuca, Arizona. Where is that anyway? I should be going to the officer career course shouldn't I? I reckon because my paper work was delayed here at the B team, there was no projection into the career course and today when Chavez called the only job available was Fort Huachuca. That should teach me to monitor my own career.

February 22, 1967 Tried to get back to camp today on an Air America flight. It left an hour early. Needless to say I missed it. I then missed the flight to Nhon Co by three minutes.

So I said "to Hell with it" and got my swimsuit and went to the south china beach. The scent of salt air blowing off the bay, the sound of palms ruffling in the wind, and the pleasant sensation of warm sand oozing between my toes was a refreshing contrast to grueling weeks in the Central Highlands. I lost all track of the war as I snorkeled in the South China Sea.

That evening ate Chinese food downtown with Lieutenant Bruch, my executive officer. We had stuffed crab with cheese, shrimp and a sweet and sour sauce, and Chinese noodle soup. We ate at Francoise. However we stayed past our time and noticed all the Americans left and the VC started coming in. We got a little uncomfortable so we left.

February 23, 1967 Flew from Nha Trang to Tan Rai to say good-by, write my final OPSUM (Operational Summary) and pick up my suitcase.

The company sized unit on night operation shot one VC. The VC didn't know what hit him. I suppose they'll be confused for awhile — walking through the jungles at night and all of a sudden one falls dead. That will keep them guessing. The starlight scope is really helpful and certainly gives us the advantage at night.

I then talked the CV-2 pilots into flying me to Bao Loc. That's where I am now waiting for Colonel Johnson to return so I can fly to Buon Ma Thuot with him. My replacement informed me that Colonel Rossi said I did a great job as an A-Team Commander. It was good to hear because I felt he was the only man who didn't appreciate the way I operated because I went over his head and to hear that he thinks I did outstanding gives me pride in a job well done. I know everyone else thinks we performed miracles in a short time.

Talked to Colonel Sharp and all the gang at Bao Loc. They were concerned about a convoy coming up the Mata Gui Pass on Highway 20. The convoy is carrying a new tea-processing machine and they expected the VC to ambush the convoy. Colonel Sharp sent two battalions down, also overhead cover. Captain Wesby found the long lost bulldozer. Charley has it building a road. The Ho Chi Minh Trail, just west of us.

February 24, 1967 Tui Ta (Major) Dieu presented me with the Vietnamese Cross of Gallantry today, with Silver Star. He gathered his LLDB and a few Strikers together and conducted a formal ceremony. The Vietnamese seem to take pride in these formalities and ceremonies. I was proud to receive this heroism award. I'm sitting here at New Buon Ma Thuot, East field with Master Sergeant "Mac" Williamson waiting to go to Pleiku. Mac escorted Captain Wells Cunningham's remains back to Missouri in August, per request of Colonel Patch. He was Cunningham's Operations Sergeant. The three of us worked closely together in Germany.

SECTION SIX: MEDAL OF HONOR

February 24, 1967
(Later in the day)
Just found out the convoy was attacked down in Lam
Dong. I heard reports of two VC companies. Also a little
action in Nha Trang yesterday. Seems like lately just after
I leave a place the action starts. Darn! I miss all the fun.
Here I am in Pleiku. It seems the place has changed.
However, the same Vietnamese are still working here.
They all recognized me before I recognized them. Saw
lots of old friends but for the most part everyone has
already rotated back to the states. The Mike Force here is
on their way to rescue elements of the 4th Infantry
Division. Also, listen to this—Bao Loc got overrun today.
They've been fighting there all day. The 101st will go in
and rescue the situation also other ARVN units. So far
the VC haven't done anything around Tan Rai. I expect
Tan Rai will get mortared tonight or probed. I'd sure like
to be there. Town fighting would be a blast and a new
experience for me. Nothing would please me more.
Went to a party at the Mike Force shack as Captain Clyde
Sincere's guest. He told me about some of his escapades.
We laughed.
February 25, 1967 Started for Nha Trang at 1400 hours.
Finally after stopping at An Khe, Qui Nhon and Cam
Rhan Bay we made it to Nha Trang. Got shot at once
while leaving Pleiku. Only one round hit the wing.
Couldn't do much paper processing and clearing because
it was late when we arrived. Took in a movie: "Battle of
the Bulge".

Mistake: it wasn't Bao Loc that was overrun, but Di Linh. My good friend Captain Wilbanks was killed in action yesterday. Shot out of the sky in his O1E Birddog single engine aircraft. He saved a Vietnamese Ranger Company from getting ambushed. (Later found out he received the MOH) Hilliard Wilbanks, a great friend. We flew many hours together. He was a fantastic pilot and a sincere good man.

February 26, 1967 Cleared Fifth Special Forces Group this morning. I was surprised it didn't take longer, in spite of the fact everyone had to sign my clearance papers. Went to Charley Diep's store, my contractor, to say good-bye and received a parting gift for Heidi (Vietnamese shoes) and a Tiger claw encased in gold. Since I could not accept a gift for myself, I accepted the two gifts on behalf of Heidi and Alexander. Ate at Francoise. This time I did not want to chance it so I ate early before the VC came in. I cleared along side a Lieutenant who came in country with me a year ago, John E. Strait. He was on an A-Team at Tan Chau, A-428, for twelve months. My buddy from Germany, Jim Miles, was the commander. We had a lot to talk about. I think I told everyone in the world good-bye now, so I'm ready to take off. Went to the aerial port to get transportation and found out they had me flying on the wrong date. I'm never going to get out of this place.

February 27, 1967 Finalized clearing, picked up awards, signed out and went to Air America to wait for a ride. Finally got to Saigon in a C7-A. Saw Sergeant Major Jim Shoulders, my team sergeant from Germany. A most Charismatic leader he was the best in Europe and his men respected him immensely. He is being medically evacuated to Tokyo.

February 28, 1967 I am manifested on flight T740Y leaving Bien Hoa March 1st at 1045 hours. Saigon is quiet and off limits. We got in about 1900 hours last night, so just had time to eat and sleep. Was a restful night.

Stayed at Long Bien. Saw Captain Dave Vozka, my old summer camp buddy from Fort Riley Kansas. Summer Camp seems so long ago. He reminded me that I had received #1 standing in Platoon, #1 in Company and #2 at the Regimental (Camp) level and Vietnam was easy compared to those accomplishments. I had to disagree. Ironically, I found out later, my roommate in Germany Robb Rowe was also number one at Fort Riley in his school category while I was number one in my school category. I believe he was from Wisconsin University. Processed with not much effort and as it turned out was a very enjoyable event, knowing where I was going.

CHAPTER 16 END OF TOUR

March 1, 1967 Last day in Vietnam
Up at 0500 hours, I can't believe it, USA, here I come,
land of the big PX. Left Saigon around 1130 hours. Ann
Margaret was on the plane but no one paid any attention
to her, nor she to us. We were all sleeping shortly after
take off. We lifted straight up from the Tan Son Nhut
airport. Before dozing off, I was thinking of my buddy,
Wells Cunningham. Why did he have to die? I was
thinking of the Village chief and all the team members
who had been at Tan Rai during the critical building
phase. I also thought of the new members taking over
and so eager to do the right thing. I especially thought of
my buddy Wilbanks, who was always willing to risk his
life for the team members and me when we were in
trouble. I really felt empty that he was killed. I lost a
part of me when these people died. He, like Wells, was
such a good human being. Then I thought of the
magnitude of the Congressional Medal of Honor that
was bestowed upon Wilbanks posthumously. Damn if
he could have only lived to strut around and wear it. We
are friends forever.

Appendices 1-9

Appendix 1 Summary of Operations February 1967

My Final Monthly Operational Summary Feb 67 Tan Rai
A-232
Here is my actual Monthly Operational Summary for
February 1967,
1. General: VNSF Commander is Lt. Tho Truong Nguyen
with 2 officers 8 enlisted, Myself as commander of
USASF with 2 officers and 8 enlisted; Company 261 has
75, Company 262 has 81, 263 has 71, 264 has 75, Recon
has 43, Arty has 20 Hq has 4 for a total of 369
Montagnards.
Number of desertions this period 24 with 4 VN and 18
K'ho, 1 Tai and 1 Rhade.
2. Highlights for the month include;
a. The month of February started off with the Tan Rai
Camp supporting the operation "Gatling One". Two
companies from the camp participated. One company
served as blocking force and the other company acted as
security for an artillery unit from the 101st Airborne
Division. This operation started on February 1st and
ended on February 4th, 1967. The 101st Airborne, several
Mike Force companies, and the CIDG from Tan Rai
participated in this operation. VC initiated contacts,
usually squad size, are made when our operational units
approach larger VC elements. VC knowledge of our
Med-Evac procedures and the time involved allows the
VC force to disperse. VC activity in this area has
increased since TET.

b. Prior to TET, the general movement of VC elements was to the North. Since TET, the general movement of VC elements has been to the South. VC propaganda has been stressing the assassination of the Americans and the harming of the families of the CIDG. The quality of the VC propaganda has improved since TET.

c. The Civic Action Program has produced very favorable results. VC suspects are being picked up based on information from the villagers. The security element deployed at Minrong Sekang, has caused the villagers to assist in our intelligence effort. An improvement was made at the CIDG Village dispensary with the addition of an autoclave for sterilizing instruments. Several latrines were constructed at the village. Hygiene classes were given to the children. The villagers also have a new burn pit for waste material. The villagers seem very appreciative of our efforts to improve their village.

d. Camp construction has continued with the improvement of the mortar positions. Sidewalks have been constructed in the preparation for the coming monsoon season. Improvements in the supply room are almost complete with the construction of an office and arms room. Due to the dry season, a new road will be constructed to the nearest water point. This will save time and effort in obtaining water. A wash point will be built in the camp to eliminate the washing of equipment at the creek, which results in equipment loss. Information has been forwarded to higher headquarters concerning the condition of the runway. A new dispensary is planned for inside the camp.

3. PROBLEM AREAS AND RECOMMENDATIONS:

a. When a change in personnel is made at a staff level, a thorough briefing should be given to the new person. They should become familiar with the contents of their files and materials. On occasions, requirements have come down requesting material that was submitted the previous month and is still valid. The new staff member's knowledge of his material on hand might eliminate a few of the non-periodic reports that the A-Det is required to submit. This is not intended to indicate that we don't appreciate the problems encountered at the B team staff level, due to transportation problems.

4. TIPS OF THE TRADE:

a. The use of the 4.2 Mortar boxes for the manufacture of concrete blocks was successful. By placing a divider in the box, two blocks can be made. These blocks are good for steps and will serve to build as well.

b. Tan Rai Camp is using the Starlight Scopes on operations and is working on improving techniques in their use. They are extremely effective in detection of personnel on the trails at night.

ANNEX B OPERATIONAL STATISTICS

1. Number of CIDG operations conducted; Combat Platoons initiated 56 day and 57 night operations for a total of 113. Reconnaissance Platoons 38 day and 46 night operations. Ambushes 84 day and night. For a total of 364 operations.

4. VC LOSSES: (CONFIRMED)

Two KIA and Five suspects.

5. FRIENDLY LOSSES:

One CIDG WIA.

Appendix 2 Written by Chuck Orona, Team Medic

(This musing was written by Chuck Orona about his first enemy contact at Tan Rai. His recollection of the date is slightly different than mine.)

by Chuck Orona

Dear Ray; This is all very rough and slow in coming but I have to fight with the kid and Candy for computer time. Also received the photo today. I recognize the outlaws.

16 September 1966

I woke in an alien world. One moment I was sleeping peacefully, the next I was thrust into the most hideous cacophony of sound I had ever known. I was certain it was the end of my world.

Sgt. Vanhorne had also woke me at 0200 that same morning. I too had been a participant in the previous evening's festivities. And so it was that at that ungodly hour I was unsuccessfully trying to locate equipment, such salient items as my rifle and necessary ammunition, and a suitable means for carrying all these items. To say I was unprepared would be like saying – I was caught on the commode.

The preparations for this fiasco are mercifully a blur with the exception of Vanhorne's incessant laugh. Thank goodness, he had seen to provisions for "Delta's Darlings", as I would come to know them. These "darlings" were so named because the mean age of "D Company, CIDG, A-232" was approximately 14 years old. Vanhorne was their mentor and this was the first time since he had arrived on site they would venture beyond the gate as a fighting force without his guidance. I would, over the course of the next year, become very familiar with all of these men and their families.

My next recollection of that ill fated morning was that of crossing a swamp filled with chest deep water and having no recollection of where I was, where I was headed, or even if I was with the right group of people. Thank goodness, for the fact they knew where they were headed and how things were really supposed to be in the real war.

I traveled in this fog for several hours and was happy for the rest when the unit stopped to eat and send out ambush patrols. Upon learning we would remain in this area several hours, I made myself comfortable and, as any good soldier would do, I fell asleep. (SFC Gerald Howland, Med. Ops. NCO for the 6th SPG at Ft. Bragg, had once found me napping one afternoon in the medical supply area in an impossible position. His comment then was of amazement, and was to the fact "A good soldier can sleep anywhere.") I was to find this ability would be of much comfort to me in the next 20 years.

My next insertion into my world occurred in the opening paragraph in this story. My brain kicked into gear with the rest of my being and I realized what I was hearing was gunfire and a lot of it. My first thought was to defend myself as I was certain from the proximity and volume of gunfire we were being overrun by the intruders. Unfortunately, in my haste to repair the damage I had done to my body the day before, I was unable to find, first of all, my glasses. Now this may not seem like a big deal, but imagine trying to identify an enemy (let alone a friend) with 20/400 vision. The second big concern was my inability to rapidly locate what was to become my best friends, my rifle, and web gear. I suppose it took no longer than twenty or thirty seconds to locate all three items, but I was certain at the time my life was hanging in the balance.

By some stroke of luck, I was finally able to locate all the necessary paraphernalia of war, and was ready to do my duty as I had been sworn to do. Unfortunately, it was at about this same time all the CIDG began yelling in a manner which did nothing to dispel my notion we had been overrun by a vastly superior enemy force. I looked to my leader, (Captain Striler) to see what action he would take with this impending hand-to-hand battle. I was amazed to see him calmly talking to camp on our FM radio and giving a SITREP (situation report). How could anyone be that cool and collected in the face of impending doom?

Striler finally stopped talking on the radio long enough to shout (from a distance of about thirty feet) instruction for me to go find out what all the shooting and shouting was about. Hell, I was the rookie but I knew doom and destruction when I heard it. (Later in my career I was to be subjected to intense rocket and mortar barrages which was my real introduction to the world of advanced warfare) Not wanting to seem lacking, I began the trek to where the firing now seemed to be centered. Guiding myself on the volume of noise, I slowly made my way to the outer perimeter of our company defense. To this day, I have the most vivid recollection of a pine tree twenty feet to my right front being severed about two feet above ground and slowly toppling to the ground after being struck by a burst of gunfire. I had to force myself to continue.

I was met at the perimeter of the defense by one of the Delta Company CIDG Officers who immediately began relaying instructions, requests, information, and God knows what other tidbits to me. Unfortunately, everything he was saying was in the Koho dialect and if you were to ask my name in English at that moment, I wouldn't have had been able to formulate an answer. His superior knowledge at that moment was wasted on me. I did note a casualty being carried in my direction and this was something I did or at least was supposed to know about. At my direction, the casualty was transported to the company headquarters for further care and disposition. The company medics (CIDG) expertly applied bandages while Captain Striler gave an injection of morphine and did all the right things to reassure the wounded soldier. He also made a request for a helicopter to dust off the wounded and it seemed as if everything happened in record time. I had only heard horror stories of wounded being forced to lie around for days waiting transportation. This did not seem to be the case here. This first exposure to combat was a true rite of passage for me.

I learned many valuable lessons on that first day. Probably the first was not to do stupid things. I saved drinking for more appropriate occasions and places. Secondly, my web gear, rifle, and glasses were on my person at all times. I determined I could survive without the pack containing food and miscellaneous items, but everything I needed was always on my person. Only one time was I ever separated from my glasses again and that was several years later when the concussion from a B-40 rocket knocked me to the ground and I was unable to locate my glasses.

I also became more attuned to the sounds of war and the people who were fighting it. I learned that experience did not lessen the fear normal humans feel while engaged in a shooting war. In fact, the knowledge of what could and did occur in a shooting war seemed to heighten the fear in all of us. The biggest struggle was to overcome the battle inside to conquer this fear.

Appendix 3 Letter from Wells Cunningham

(Wells and I were roommates at Pleiku prior to his assignment as camp commander at Duc Co in April 1966. This is a note from Wells to me.)

Duc Co, Viet Nam 12 April 1966

Dear Ray,

As per usual, a few moments of reflection has led me to remember quite a few things that I should have taken care of before I left camp. First and foremost, I'm enclosing coins in various currency which amounts to roughly $100. What I'd like you to do is buy a money order and make it payable to Bruce Emery and mail it to him. You will find his address in a little green memo book either in my half of the wall locker or on our dresser. He's at Fort Jackson.

Next, I hope you can pick up the sleeping jacket from the tailors and get it out to me soon. Plus, I'd like these following items: A few scrounged pair of tiger suits. This shouldn't be all that hard, particularly if you check with Lt. Pinkerton, whom I readily acknowledge as a scrounger without peer. Next, my combat boots. Both pair. You can shove them in the duffel bag you'll find on top of the wall locker. Then, of course, I'll need as many of the books in my wall locker as you can get out to me. In particular, the big book of Kipling you'll find on the top shelf, and the Seven Story Mountain by Mertom. Please stuff in my Pajamas laying on the chair there, and anything you may think I'll need.

I tell you, Ray, it's strange. One moment, I'm carrying around a FM 101-5 Staff manual and the next minute, I'm C.O. of my first combat command. Strangely enough, I feel remarkably calm. I've walked the camp perimeter, and at first light in the morning, I'll get out and really get read in on the place. There is a move afoot to recover Conway's body, and depending how the route of the recovery troops shapes up, I may be on that. From the map, it will be hairy as hell. They surely suspect we'll be coming back and the terrain is all Charlie's way. I can't get over how calm I feel. It is exactly as if I was almost expecting this. My mind seems to be functioning in a remarkably school-like manner, and while I by no means feel smug or cocky, I feel grimly confident that I have things in hand.

One thing of course, while I don't intend to make any great changes initially things will change. Conway and I are nearly poles apart in our manner. I couldn't be Conway if I tried and I'd be a fool to try. Well, it shall be a very interesting task and I shall do my best.

I appreciate you helping me out with my affairs like this, and in getting me packed up to catch my plane. Although I noticed to my simultaneous chagrin and amusement that you let me walk out with my pistol belt on upside down. Still and all, I like to think those about me perhaps lacked my keen powers of perception so it's possible nobody else noticed it.

Oh yes. Also shove in a few magazines to read. Playboys and what not. The three what-nots I gave you as I was leaving. Once you've read them of course, I bought them in San Francisco just before I left and never have got around to reading them.

Well, buddy, take care, and thanks again. I shall do my best to keep you informed. You may even be better informed than the good Colonel Patch, as he would be obliged to court martial me if I told him everything I'd tell you. And incidentally, I have reason to believe I'll become an excellent source of enemy small arms soon. You trading fiend, you. One of our units captured six SKS weapons today, Makes one's mouth watery doesn't it?

Oh yes, please check with Sergeant Major Davis on the matter of the B-25 team party. The EM in the B team work very hardy and are in dire need of a party and a little getting over. I'll greatly appreciate it if you can help them out. You lucky C teamers don't quite appreciate the six day week you have and the bliss of sleeping late on the Sabbath and sun-bathing and all.

Buy bonds,
Signed Wells

p.s. There is a FM on 60 mm Mortars in the wall locker. This goes to SFC Miles. Very important. Give him my thanks.
W.

On the envelope there is another note;
"Add a note of explanation to Bruce."

Appendix 4 MOH Captain Hilliard A. Wilbanks

(Wilbanks Medal of Honor took place just after I left Tan Rai and was in Nha Trang processing when I heard the news, I was ready to go back to help but it was too late. The location of the ambush was near Di Linh and the tea plantation I talk about in the Diary. Later Ned McGonagle and I found Wilbanks on the Vietnam Wall in Washington DC. Panel 15E-Row 088.

The President of the United States in the name of The Congress takes pleasure in presenting the Medal of Honor to

*WILBANKS, HILLIARD A.

Rank and organization: Captain, U.S. Air Force, 21st. Tactical Air Support Squadron, Nha Trang AFB, RVN. Place and Date: Near Dalat, Republic of Vietnam, 24 February 1967. Entered service at: Atlanta, Ga. Born: 26 July 1933, Cornelia, Ga.

Citation:

For conspicuous gallantry and intrepidity in action at the risk of his life above and beyond the call of duty. As a forward air controller Capt. Wilbanks was pilot of an unarmed, light aircraft flying visual reconnaissance ahead of a South Vietnam Army Ranger Battalion. His intensive search revealed a well-concealed and numerically superior hostile force poised to ambush the advancing rangers. The Viet Cong, realizing that Capt. Wilbanks' discovery had compromised their position and ability to launch a surprise attack, immediately fired on the small aircraft with all available firepower. The enemy then began advancing against the exposed forward elements of the ranger force which were pinned down by devastating fire. Capt. Wilbanks recognized that close support aircraft could not arrive in time to enable the rangers to withstand the advancing enemy, onslaught. With full knowledge of the limitations of his unarmed, unarmored, light reconnaissance aircraft, and the great danger imposed by the enemy's vast firepower, he unhesitatingly assumed a covering, close support role. Flying through a hail of withering fire at treetop level, Capt. Wilbanks passed directly over the advancing enemy and inflicted many casualties by firing his rifle out of the side window of his aircraft. Despite increasingly intense antiaircraft fire, Capt. Wilbanks continued to completely disregard his own safety and made repeated low passes over the enemy to divert their fire away from the rangers. His daring tactics successfully interrupted the enemy advance, allowing the rangers to withdraw to safety from their perilous position. During his final courageous attack to protect the withdrawing forces, Capt. Wilbanks was mortally wounded and his bullet-riddled aircraft crashed between the opposing forces. Capt. Wilbanks' magnificent action saved numerous friendly personnel from certain injury or death. His unparalleled concern for his fellow man and his extraordinary heroism were in the highest traditions of the military service, and have reflected great credit upon himself and the U.S. Air Force.

Appendix 5 Fort Benning Officers Advanced Course Nov 1968

I've met and talked to several soldiers from my A-Team at Tan Rai. They all thought it was the most sensational time of their lives. We were successful, hard working, sincere and proud of our accomplishments. We were there during a time of building. After I left it was a time of turning the camp over to ARVN. That was accomplished in 1969 when the camp was turned over to Regional and Popular Forces. The day I departed camp, Di Linh was overrun. Major Graney was killed. Captain Wilbanks was shot out of the sky. He was awarded the Medal of Honor, posthumously. He flew in the face of 50-caliber machine gun fire and antiaircraft fire, He flew directly into the VC ambush in order to warn the ARVN Ranger Battalion of an impending ambush. He saved many lives but paid the ultimate price. Captain Joe Marcelli after returning from R&R had an interesting story to tell. While surrounded by VC he evaded while shooting a few of them now and then as he evaded thus preventing his own capture or death.

I saw Captain Chet Jones, our Executive Officer, and Sergeant Chuck Orona, our Medic. Jones is now on his way back to Nam. Orona and I went hunting this morning. Ironically we were not as successful with the deer as we were with the Viet Cong.

I did not want to kill anything that could not defend itself anyhow. I just enjoyed talking to someone who shared many of the same experiences. He got fed up with OCS and volunteered for Nam again.

I told him it wouldn't be the same. He feared I was right. I've seen most of the people I mentioned in the diary upon my return. Jim Richie, promoted to Major, came to Fort Huachuca, Arizona to see us. After talking to many people, I concluded that Camp Tan Rai was undoubtedly one of the most successful Special Forces Camps in Vietnam.

Colonel John C. Bennett, now a Brigadier General, is stationed in Alaska, It was great to receive a letter from him a few weeks back.

I learned many things during my tenure as a Special Forces A-Team Commander. I don't have the writing ability to express it, but the experience is in my heart and soul forever.

When I look around at my contemporaries, I believe my experiences were valuable for me and gave me that extra strength and knowledge of what I can do if pushed to the limits. I was faced with more lightening speed 'life and death' decisions than the average person and for that I am a better person at that age and can contribute much more to society.

In retrospect I wouldn't change a thing.

Dai Uy Minh, my first counterpart, is attending the Career Course here. I first ran into him in May of 1968. His wife and children were killed in a jeep that ran over a mine. What a tragedy. He has since remarried. His Executive Officer, Tui Ta, was killed in Tay Ninh Province on an operation.

Appendix 6 Rider College 1983 Professor of Military Science

After my 1968 entry, I volunteered to serve another tour in Vietnam; this time with an American unit, No Montagnards, No Vietnamese only Americans. I served mostly in the Delta Region. I had the fortune to command a battalion for a short time, while my boss was away. I lead a battalion of infantrymen into Cambodia during the incursion of May 1970. I flew across familiar territory coming up from the delta flying over Bao Loc, Tan Rai, Nhon Co, An Lac and into the staging area of Duc Lap. In Cambodia we located fifty-eight large weapon caches on 'Shakey's Hill'. I mean the size of a small room five meters by five. I began to understand the formidable enemy just over the border in Cambodia where we were restricted from going. Meanwhile back at home Kent State University shootings were making headlines during May of 1970. Americans wanted out of Vietnam. I did not hear about Kent State until I returned from Vietnam.

An update of the 20 November 1968 entry is as follows. General Bennett was a two-star General when he retired. He assisted Alexander Haig while Haig was President Nixon's Executive Officer. Bennett died in an aircraft accident.

Dai Uy Minh and I had a long talk in 1969 while he was at my home in Fort Benning Georgia for dinner. He basically felt the U.S. and USSR were fueling the war in Vietnam and the Americans should get out. I was shocked to hear that from him. When I returned to VN in 1969-70 I found this same attitude among the South Vietnamese leadership. They lost their will to fight. They were tired, families split and bewildered. They had enough.

Sergeant Bobby Clark, our radioman, is now Sergeant Major Clark, I saw him at Fort Bragg in 1982.

Lieutenant Colonel Simpson wrote a book entitled, "Inside the Green Berets". I saw him at Fort Bragg 1983 and he autographed the book for me.

I heard follow up stories on Captain Wells Cunningham. Seems as though Colonel Joe McDonnell was the Survivor Assistant Officer and Sergeant Major Mac Williamson was the Survival Assistance NCO. McDonnell, my Battalion commander in 1975 told me, "Yes, Cunningham had a $100,000 insurance policy divided among three women, Mia Unterberg, (Germany's Unterberg Bitters Family) was one and the other lady was one from the USA, whom I met in Germany and the other, McDonnell could not remember. And yes, Cunningham requested to be buried in his one of a kind limousine black Mercedes, however this request was not granted.

The chopper pilot who med-evac'd me to Nha Trang, notified his German wife who lived in Reichersbeuern, Germany, where my wife was staying while I was in VN. The pilot told his wife a few days after I was wounded. It's a small world; his wife saw mine in downtown Bad Tölz and asked,

"How is your husband doing? I heard he was shot?" Needless to say, my wife had not been told until then and was distraught with worry for two weeks until she received my letter that I had written from the Hospital in Nha Trang on Red Cross stationary. In the letter I told Heidi I had a minor wound and was back at work.

Sergeant Roger Templar went to OCS and became an officer. Sergeant Eugene Tafoya was charged with an attempted assassination of an Iranian in Colorado Springs, Colorado. This event made the national news because he was accused of being one of Khadafi's hit men. He remained silent throughout the trial and was given a jail sentence. Several books have been written about Tafoya.

Appendix 7 First Mission in Combat Zone

~~CONFIDENTIAL~~

DETACHMENT C-2
5TH SPECIAL FORCES GROUP (ABN), 1ST SPECIAL
FORCES
APO US FORCES 96295

16 April 1966

SUBJECT: Convoy After Action Report

TO: Commanding Officer
             Detachment C-2, 5th SFGA
             ATTN: S-3
             APO US Forces 96295

1. Mine
2. 151030 April 1966
3. Mike Force, Nung Force
4. (a) Four platoons of Mike Force
    (b) One platoon of Nung Force
5. (a) Mike Force — 180 personnel
    (b) Nung Force — 30 personnel
9. Two CIDG with superficial wounds in upper extremities
10. None
11. One ¾ ton truck rendered inoperative: left rear wheel and housing blown off.
12. Mission was to deliver the Mike Force to Camp Plei Me. The dirt road on which the accident occurred was the only road to Camp Plei Me.
13. Armament:

(a) On the way to Camp Plei Me: 7 — M79's; 2 — 30 cal MGs; and individual small arms.

(b) On the return trip: 2 — M79s; individual weapons.

14. N/A

15. (a) One reconnaissance platoon seven kilometers away.

(b) FAC overhead.

16. None

17. (a) On the way to Camp Plei Me: 4 — ANPRC 25s; 12 — HT-1s.

(b) On the return trip: 1 — ANPRC 25; 7 — HT-1s.

18. (a) FAC overhead

(b) Plei Me 14 kilometers to the South

(c) Relay to Det C-2 via FAC

19. None

20. (a) M-79   100 each

(b) 5.56   200 each

21. Yes. One improvised mine was placed on left track moving south approximately six inches below surface. It was detonated under pressure.

22. One mine detonated

23. Only known device in the area

24. Deployment was quick and effective. After initial deployment, the MIKE Force screened the flanks as the column moved slowly toward Camp Plei Me.

25. Sparsely defoliated with few fox holes and punji stake fields nearby.

26. Captain Striler, 1/Lt Hanson, l/Lt Davis, SFC Prusinski, SPC Quinn, Sgt Watson, Sp4 Terry and SFC Nugent.

SUMMARY OF OPERATION

1. At 150930 April 1966, a convoy departed Detachment C-2, Pleiku, with 9 USSF, 180 CIDG, 30 Nungs, 11 civilian drivers and one interpreter. The mission was to deliver 180 Mike Force and 4 USSF to Camp Plei Me. Furthermore, on the return trip, the convoy was to pick up thirteen POWs and return them to Detachment C-2 LLDB.

2. At 151030 April 1966 at grid coordinates ZA220232, the second vehicle in the column (a ¾ ton truck) ran over and detonated a mine. The first seven vehicles immediately stopped and deployed. The remaining four were prepared to move in

any direction. Forward Air Control reported nothing in the area.

3. The Mike Force screened the flanks and the column started moving again slowly. The column moved making reconnaissance by fire, driving around one punji field and through another. After seven kilometers the convoy joined the Plei Me security platoon, mounted and moved rapidly to Camp Plei Me, arriving there at 1330 hours.

4. The exchange was made. The convoy departed at 1400 hours with 20 POWs.

5. On the return trip, the convoy moved at a steady pace continuing reconnaissance by fire.

6. The truck was recovered on the return trip and dragged back to Pleiku.

7. The convoy closed in Pleiku at 1630 hours.

s/Raymond J. Striler
RAYMOND J. STRILER
Captain Infantry
Convoy Commander

Appendix 8 What happened to the men of Tan Rai

1) Written 1994, Carlsbad California; Where are they now?

Sergeant Major Bobby Clark retired in 1989 and is a successful businessman today living with his lovely wife in Michigan.

Doc Chuck Orona went on to become a Physician Assistant and is much in demand today among the medical communities. He is married to a Major in the Air Force, Candy. They have a teenage daughter.

Sergeant Major Jim Nabors retired in 1986 started his second career in the Post office and after rising to an exalted rank retired in Fort Bragg North Carolina.

Colonel Bud Gillette retired in 1980 opened a successful business in Chili, reached second retirement and is now working with his Chilean wife Marta at their business in Florida.

Ed McGonagle earned his Baccalaureate degree majoring in English. He then chose a radio and TV career. He is now located in the Boston area.

Clyde Sincere is working for Vinell Corporation, hiring personnel to work in Saudi Arabia.

SFC Coon wounded and evacuated to Japan in March 67. He died too early.

Ludwig Faistenhammer retired from a second career in a major Corporation.

Bob Shepherd, went on to have a full career as a very successful jet pilot for Delta. Retired in early 90's living in Newport Beach California. He invested in property and did well. He looks great and keeps himself in great shape.

Mac Williamson points to Rolex while tears well up in his eyes.

Cunningham Gymnasium at U of Mo was named after Wells Cunningham. A.J. "Bo" Baker as a Major served Vietnam until October 66 as Commander of B-55. He later commanded SF in Germany and had a fatal heart attach after playing handball with my brother in law, Jim Humphries. Humphries wrote a descriptive book on company operations in I Corps Vietnam.

Colonel William Patch made two stars and died too early.

Jack Kistler is teaching school in Virginia.

Ola L. Mize, who received the MOH in Korea before coming command Bon Ea Yang, was later promoted to Colonel.

2) Written 1998, Carlsbad California; Where are they now?

I have been in touch with Ned McGonagle, Bob Tink (Nhon-Co), Roger Donlon, James G. "Jim" Miles (Commander Tan Chau A-428 DEROS May 67), Bud Gillette, Jim Richie, Jack Kistler, Chet Jones, David Aleo, Bo Gritz, Bob Kvederas, Bruch, Chet Jones, Dai Uy Minh. I see where Eugene Tafoya passed away on June 22, 1997, Colonel Blackjack Kelly passed away December 26, 1998, and Colonel Jerry Sage in 1993.

My good friend Chuck Orona, whom I admired so much and to whom this book is dedicated, finally succumbed to cancer from Agent Orange. Chuck Orona served several years in Vietnam in defoliated areas. He passed on quietly and peacefully, leaving a wonderful family behind. We all miss him severely. He was such a positive influence on everyone and touched many lives being a consummate empathetic Physicians Assistant. Chuck "Bac Xi" will be remembered always.

Read Jim Miles book "Pay any Price" brought back memories. It is a work of art and emotion. Way to go Jim! Read Gail Hosking Gilberg's book "Snake's Daughter" was an emotional trip, helping me remember those that had the most difficult part, staying behind while their men fought in Vietnam. Ned McGonagle and I walked the Wall in Washington DC reminiscing and asking why were we walking while our buddies were in the wall? We took eerie pictures with our reflection in the wall, maybe that's where we were supposed to be. Le Ly Hayslip's book "When heaven and earth changed places" was an eye opener. Oliver Stone made a movie of it called, 'Heaven and Earth'. I do hope her brother, the NVA soldier, will write his book. It is about a family split in war on an emotional roller coaster. She was raped by the VC, married a GI, lived happily and opulently in Rancho Sante Fe, near me here in Carlsbad California and made the best of life that was dealt her. She returns to Vietnam on hospital tours volunteering her time and money. Some in Orange County still see her as the enemy.

Appendix 9 Trip back to Vietnam after 30 years

REVISITING TAN RAI 1998
(This was published in 'Destination Vietnam' Magazine, August 1998)

Vet Returns After Thirty Years
by Ray Striler, Ed.D.

Just the thought of going back to Vietnam after 30 years conjures up intrigue, a sense of duty, mission, purpose and a desire to help the oppressed. I could not pass up the opportunity when my good friend Dr. Son Nguyen, a wonderful human being on a meaningful quest in his life, suggested that I go just two short months ago. He makes it possible for poor and deserving students to get into college. He builds universities and by the way he is a Minister. Dr. Son introduced me to my guide, Xe Truong, which proved a great omen for my visit. Spiritual, knowledgeable, personable and empathetic, Xe kept me out of trouble and exposed me to the parts of the country and population that I wanted to see based on my previous tours. Xe was a walking university with his vast experience and wisdom. He made me feel like a dignitary, as he opened doors and introduced me to everyone: peasants, university professors, presidents, minister directors and tribal people. He treated all of them with equal respect.

Things are different and yet they are the same. There is no infrastructure. There is "before 1975" and "after 1975," and poverty everywhere. Half the population was born after 1975 and has no memory of war. When I asked them at the university what they would do in 5-10 years, they had to think about it because it isn't an issue.

They just go with the flow. Speaking of going with the flow, to my amazement, there are no traffic jams. Do you know why? Because everyone from the teenage beauty in an Ao Dai on her bicycle along side the large bus moves in traffic by feel. Horns blow, they converge at the intersection and emerge out the other side unscathed. It's fascinating. Even though there are one-way traffic signs, no one pays attention to them. The key is to keep moving no matter which direction. Someone will make room for you. The Cyclos and motorbikes still outnumber vans and cars as the traffic meanders smoothly. I thought to myself, if one could figure out why the traffic flowed so effortlessly, they could build a university or start a business in Vietnam. You could get into the mindset by moving with the flow, going with the spirit just like the traffic.

Xe picked me up at Tan Son Nhat airport May 6th 1998 at noon. We made our way along with the Cyclos and bikes and motorbikes down Duong Cach Mang Thang Tam toward Dong Khoi Street (Tu Do Street) and parallel to Pasteur Street to 41 Dong Du Street in the District One. There stands the large, white Saigon Hotel in the center of Ho Chi Minh City. It's a great location, a few minutes from the Saigon River, the Saigon market, the Opera House and there are lots of shopping opportunities. The people are so friendly. They want to speak to Americans. They have seen the Russians go away taking everything in the early 90s. They have seen the migration of the poor northern peoples onto their land. Now they see the Americans coming again and they love it. It was hot and muggy except for Lam Dong Province in the Central Highlands where it was cool and lush. The people are poor all over and struggling for their existence. Tribal people have moved to areas they can farm and have given up their nomadic ways.

The forest in Lam Dong is endowed with rare and valuable flora and fauna, however these areas were diminishing rapidly at one point. The current policies have reversed this trend and the communities and government are working together to preserve the remaining forested areas.

I had a great time roaming over the province by car and on motorbike. It was spiritual and fun. My Special Forces Camp of the 60s, Tan Rai, was no longer there; in its place were little villages of tea farmers, migrants from the north, along with Montagnard tribal folks, the K'ho. I had tea with a retired communist police officer from Hanoi on the site of my old bunker.

It was much too quick a trip, just seven days from May 6th to the 13th. Shortly after arriving at the Saigon Hotel and showering, I wanted to walk around. There was a persistent young man who finally said he had visited California and knew where my home was, so I decided to get on his motorbike. It was a blast from the past. One-way streets be damned. We went everywhere. The humidity and heat that had embraced me upon stepping off China Airways at Tan Son Nhat was refreshingly blown by the wind in my face even though it was noticeably polluted. And why not? With five million people in that small city, celebrating its 300th anniversary, all of them are energetic, entrepreneurial and busy. I finished off the first day with a boat tour of the Saigon River. The export activity was incredible; rice, rubber, cashews and fruit. Oil was being brought off ship and stored along shore in fifty-five gallon drums and concrete cisterns. That's not to say the offshore oil wells are not producing. I saw them in Vung Tau later.

The second day was spent acclimating and visiting the War Remnants Museum, Notre Dame de Saigon, the former US Embassy, Chinatown and Thien Hau Temple. Fortuitously, I met with the Minister of Communications personnel director in Saigon and discussed internet classrooms.

The third day we drove to DaLat in the highlands stopping at a rubber, cashew, tea and coffee plantation. I observed the infamous silkworm in its stages of growth. I visited villages that I remembered from the 60s — Bao Loc and Di Linh and of course the K'ho tribal villages.

I spent the fourth day in DaLat — the Zoo, Chinese temple, Domain de Marie, the omnipresent market and DaLat University. The highlight was talking with three groups of students on campus that didn't want me to leave. They were so eager to converse in English. In fact everywhere I looked people were working, sweeping, cleaning, building, making something.

The fifth day I drove back to Saigon stopping at Tan Rai. This was the most outstanding part of my trip — to see where my old camp was. It's still hard to believe that I actually went back to Tan Rai Special Forces Camp on a motorbike where I had not been since March of 1967. I could not recognize a thing. The name had changed; folks in the area knew where the camp was located. While in 1967 it was a primeval jungle with a tea plantation and no visible population, it is now open rolling hills with resettlement villages of people from the north. Everyone was friendly and helpful; I met families, individuals, soldiers and K'ho.

On the sixth day I took a trip to Vung Tau University with colleagues. One of the professors wants to use the American education system. The government disbanded the Russian education plan that had replaced the French plan and now they are in transition, seeking new goals and concepts.

The bottom line is that they want the American curriculum, teaching methods, adult learning theory and lifelong learning concepts. They also want the internet in the classroom, which is now highly regulated and censored. It is a nation in early development of knowledge-on-demand learning and modern learning methodologies. Opportunities are infinite.

And on the seventh day I departed totally exhausted and slept all the way to LAX. I highly recommend it to any kindred spirit.

Appendix 10 The Author

About the Author

Ray Striler retired from the army in the 80"s spending half his career overseas in Germany, England and several tours in Vietnam. Colonel Striler and his wife Heidi live in Carlsbad, California.

Striler earned a Bachelor's degree from Missouri State University, a Master's degree from Peabody of Vanderbilt University, a second Master's degree from Rider University and a Doctorate from USIU under the aegis of Alliant University.

Dr. Striler has been affiliated with higher education research and consulting where he has been instrumental in facilitating educational opportunities worldwide. He founded Education 2020 Inc., a Corporation recognized for its international innovative higher education consulting. He co-founded Apollos University and retired as President.

In retirement he enjoys writing Screen Plays.

Appendix 11 Pictures

Tan Rai Camp

Team Sergeant with Village Elders

Striler is fourth from right

Tan Rai village chief and elders

Striler, Nabors, Williams, Clark back row
Wesby, Bruch, Templar, and Coon

Striker village and dependents

Strikers coming home from four-day patrol

White and Striler

General Heinkes, Westmoreland's Deputy

Original Tan Rai Village at end of runway circa 1962

Rifle shooting contest

Dividing buffalo meat. Supervised by K'Gee Commander

Province Chief and Advisor

Rice wine into mouth

Saved for VIP's

Wesby looking at mixing of blood and wine

Slusser, Jackson and Gouch looking at Dinner a Wild Boar

Wells Cunningham (KIA) and Striler

Getting ready for patrol

A-232 Tan Rai Special Forces Camp II Corps Vietnam

Shower and Ammo Bunker

Jim Nabors, TOP, with herd

McGonagle and Orona with K'ho hutch maids

Striler and Williams going on four-day operation

Vanhorne, Striler, Griffith PPSH41

Schmidt, Patch, Gen Vinh Loc II Corps, Phong

Striler, Gen Heinkes (Westmoreland's Deputy)

John C Bennett visiting me at Tan Rai (Col Kelly's Deputy) Later a MG worked for Haig, also Deputy Assistant to President Nixon, killed in airplane. My battalion commander in Germany, a brilliant great man.

Captain Wilbanks (MOH) on left McGonagle on right
Front row SFC Coon

Loin Cloth and top; K'ho Montagnard

Montagnard and Vietnamese Dress with Author

General Matheson 101st Airborne Commander with LTC Collins 1/327th Airborne Battalion, Tan Rai February 1967

Commanders Dietrick and Collins of 101st Airborne
Battalions on Tan Rai operation February 2nd 1967 Collins
on right 1/327th Abn Bn.

Author and Counterpart, Dai Uy Minh

Striler relaxing in Camp

Raymond Joseph Striler, Captain Special Forces

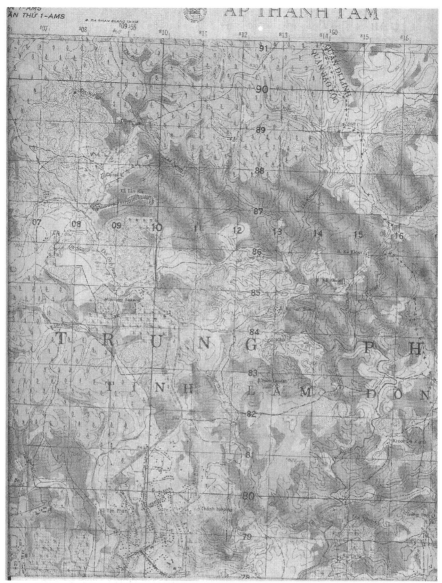

Tan Rai upper and Bao Loc lower

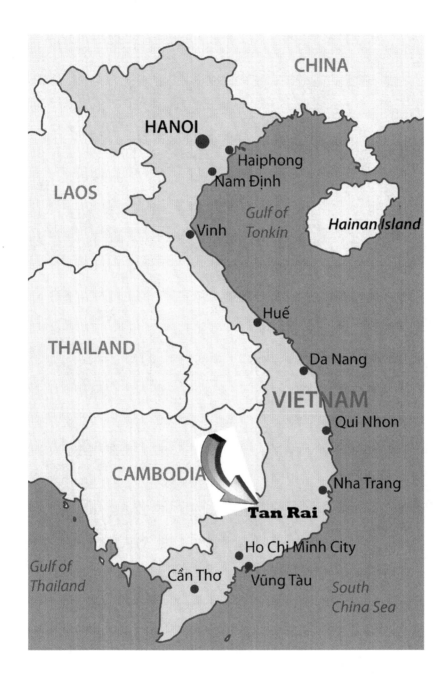

CHINA

HANOI

Haiphong

Nam Định

LAOS

Gulf of
Tonkin

Hainan Island

Vinh

THAILAND

Huế

Da Nang

VIETNAM

Qui Nhon

CAMBODIA

Nha Trang

Tan Rai

Ho Chi Minh City

Gulf of
Thailand

Cần Thơ

Vũng Tàu

South
China Sea

GLOSSARY

A-232: Tan Rai, Vietnam Special Forces A-Team

A-TEAM: Twelve men; Detachment Commander, Executive Officer, Team Sergeant, Intelligence Sergeant plus two each, Weapons, Demolitions, Medical, and Communications Sergeants. However the reality is only two or three are available in camp at any one time

AGENT ORANGE: In our AO, Agent Orange was one of the herbicides and defoliants used to clear areas for operations

AK-47: Communist 7.62 caliber, automatic assault rifle

AO DAI: Traditional Vietnamese Dress

AO: Area of Operations

ARVN: Army of the Republic of Vietnam

B-23: Buon Ma Thuot

BAC XI: Doctor

BAO LOC: Nearest large town and headquarters of Lam Dong Province

BEAUCOUP: French for "very many"

BMNT: Buon Ma Thuot is the location of the B-Team Headquarters

C-2: Pleiku is the C-Team Headquarters

C-3: Plastic explosive

CHARLIE/Chuck/Mr. Charles/VC: Name for Viet Cong or North Vietnamese Army NVA

CHIEU HOI: Surrendered VC or NVA

CIDG: Civil Irregular Defense Group

CLAYMORE MINE: Command detonated; anti-personnel mine saturates area 6 feet above ground and in area of 60 degrees with 750 steel ball bearings.

CONEX: Large Steel Container

D'TAN JA RANG: Small village near Tan Rai

DAI UY: Vietnamese for Captain

DALAT: Lâm Đồng's capital

DEROS: Date of Estimated Return from Overseas

DEUCE AND A HALF: 2.5 ton Truck

DI LINH: Village near Tan Rai where Wilbanks was brave and deadly springing ambush from the air. He crashed and resultantly received the MOH

FAC: Forward Air Controller

FOO GAS: A mixture of JP-4 aviation fuel and naphtha, buried in 55 gallon drums and placed on the outer perimeter

FREE-FIRE ZONE: Off-limits to all personnel, within which one is assumed to be hostile.

FULRO: Federation for the Liberation of the Oppressed Races

HIGHWAY 20: Major road, west to east in Lam Dong Province

HO CHI MINH TRAIL: A vast network of roads and trails, running from North Vietnam through Laos and Cambodia and terminating northwest of Saigon, extensions of which came diagonally through our AO

HUEY: UH1 Helicopter for transportation and supply

II Corps: Central Military District in South Vietnam

K'HO: The K'Ho, Cơ Ho, or Koho are our soldiers, they are the indigenous people of Lâm Đồng Province.

K'GEE: Battalion Commander

LLDB: Vietnamese Special Forces (Counterparts)

M-16: Lightweight automatic assault rifle, 5.56 Caliber

M-60: Light 7.62 belt-fed, machine gun

M-79: Single shot, 40 mm grenade launcher

MACV: Military Advisory Command, Vietnam

MEDEVAC: Helicopter conducting a medical evacuation

MIKE FORCE: A force multiplier, a reserve for A-Teams in trouble, consisting of indigenous volunteers

MONSOON: The rainy season

MOUNTAGNARD: Indigenous people of Central Highlands of Vietnam

MPC: Military Payment Certificate used by US in Vietnam

NDP: Night defensive position

NHA TRANG: Special Forces Vietnam Headquarters

NOUC MAM: Fish Sauce

NUMBER 1 AND NUMBER 10: Slang for Best and Worst

NVA: North Vietnamese Army

PF: Popular Forces, South Vietnamese irregular forces

PIASTRES: Vietnamese currency

PRC-25 OR PRICK 25: Portable radio used in the field

RF: Regional Forces

RPD: Hand held light 7.62mm machine gun

RPG: Rocket Propelled Grenade

SF: Special Forces

SFG(A): Special Forces Group (Airborne)

SPOTTER ROUND: Mortar smoke shell to mark targets or establish location

STARLIGHT SCOPE: Night vision device utilizing ambient light such as the moon or stars finally obtained at Tan Rai at the end of my tour

TAN RAI: Our village and camp located between Saigon and Dalat in Lam Dong Province

TET: Vietnamese New Year

WILLIE PETER: White phosphorus

YARDS: Short for Montagnard tribesmen

INDEX

Gabriel, 121

Gillette, 8, 25, 27, 46, 48, 55, 57, 79, 81, 91, 102, 103, 104, 107, 108, 109, 111, 134, 136, 139, 142, 145, 183, 184

Grany, 143

Gritz, 184

Haig, 177

Hayslip, 185

Highway 20, 157

Ho Chi Minh Trail, 13, 157

Hosking, 185

Huey, 132

Johnson, 25, 50, 64, 86, 95, 96, 98, 121, 126, 144, 146, 147, 156

Jones, 8, 34, 35, 40, 47, 80, 87, 96, 112, 113, 132, 133, 139, 140, 141, 145, 152, 175, 184

K'ho, 12, 14, 15, 23, 32, 112, 113, 116, 162

K'Gee, 23, 40, 57, 80, 113

Ke Tan Bla, 91

Kelly, 36, 49, 94, 142, 144, 145, 184

Kennedy, 6

Kistler, 46, 99, 132, 184

Kolbe, 122

Krapfl, 17

Kvederas, 145, 184

Lam Dong, 13, 38, 66, 158

Lamar, 147

Leach, 108

LLDB, 11, 28, 29, 30, 47, 51, 54, 56, 78, 82, 100, 102, 104, 107, 109, 110, 111, 112, 115, 118, 119, 127, 139, 151, 157

Loc, 17, 33, 46, 47, 48, 56, 60, 69, 70, 88, 91, 94, 100, 101, 102, 106, 107, 108, 110, 112, 113, 119, 126, 127, 129, 132, 136, 138, 139, 140, 143, 144, 151, 153, 155, 156, 157, 158, 159, 177

M-16, 61, 63, 89, 137, 154

Mann, 155

Margaret, 161

Marlow, 136

Mata Gui, 157

Matheson, 145, 146

McDinnell, 143

McGonagle, 8, 115, 143, 150, 183, 184, 185

Mike Force, 145, 146, 158, 162

Miles, 159, 184, 185

Miller, 148, 153, 154

Made in the USA
San Bernardino, CA
15 October 2015